The Talking About BPD Workbook

by the same author

Talking About BPD
A Stigma-Free Guide to Living a Calmer, Happier Life with Borderline Personality Disorder
Rosie Cappuccino
Foreword by Kimberley Wilson
ISBN 978 1 78775 825 4
eISBN 978 1 78775 826 1
Audio ISBN 978 1 52937 104 8

of related interest

Sorry My Mental Illness Isn't Sexy Enough for You
Lessons on Living with Personality Disorders and Mental
Illness (That We Learned the Hard Way)
Katja Pavlovna and Kay Garbett
Foreword by Peter Tyrer
ISBN 978 1 80501 067 8
eISBN 978 1 80501 068 5

DBT for Everyone
A Guide to the Perks, Pitfalls, and Possibilities of DBT for Better Mental Health
Kate Sherman and Michelle Henderson
ISBN 978 1 83997 588 2
eISBN 978 1 83997 589 9
Audio ISBN 978 1 39981 632 8

The Talking About BPD Workbook

Reflections and Creative Prompts for Exploring Your Life with a Diagnosis of Borderline Personality Disorder

Rosie Cappuccino

Illustrated by Alyse Ruriani
Foreword by Imi Lo

Jessica Kingsley Publishers
London and Philadelphia

First published in Great Britain in 2026 by Jessica Kingsley Publishers
An imprint of John Murray Press

The information contained in this book is not intended to replace the services
of trained medical professionals or to be a substitute for medical advice. You
are advised to consult a doctor on any matters relating to your health, and in
particular on any matters that may require diagnosis or medical attention.

Content warning: this book mentions emotional abuse, verbal abuse, child neglect, anger issues,
anxiety, panic attacks, paranoia, misogyny, sexual abuse, sexual assault, sexual violence, self-
harm, suicide, suicidal ideation, suicidal thoughts, transphobia, trauma, PTSD, victim blaming

A CIP catalogue record for this title is available from the
British Library and the Library of Congress

ISBN 978 1 80501 409 6
eISBN 978 1 80501 410 2

Printed and bound in Great Britain by Bell & Bain Limited

Jessica Kingsley Publishers' policy is to use papers that are natural, renewable and recyclable
products and made from wood grown in sustainable forests. The logging and manufacturing
processes are expected to conform to the environmental regulations of the country of origin.

Jessica Kingsley Publishers
Carmelite House
50 Victoria Embankment
London EC4Y 0DZ

www.jkp.com

John Murray Press
Part of Hodder & Stoughton Limited
An Hachette UK Company

The authorised representative in the EEA is Hachette Ireland,
8 Castlecourt Centre, Dublin 15, D15 XTP3, Ireland (email: info@hbgi.ie)

To everyone with a diagnosis of BPD, no matter how they feel about the label, and also to those individuals who don't have a formal diagnosis but who relate to it all the same.

This book is for those of you who have been told that you feel too much, cry too much, laugh too much, think too much, talk too much, are too much.

It's for those of you trapped between the desire to speak about your experiences and the fear of what such honesty may bring.

It's for anyone who has been kicked whilst they're down and felt grateful for scraps of care... but who deserves so much more.

I hope this book helps you see your worth, your strengths and that you deserve nothing less than the utmost respect, support and understanding.

Contents

Foreword

I was truly honoured and moved when Rosie Cappuccino invited me to introduce *The Talking About BPD Workbook*. Reading Rosie's book, you immediately feel you are in compassionate and knowledgeable hands. It is a rare gift to find a resource that speaks so directly and helpfully to the experience of borderline personality disorder (BPD). Here, Rosie has created one that blends lived wisdom, heartfelt understanding and solid research.

BPD is one of the most heavily stigmatized and misunderstood diagnoses in psychology. In a world that often makes people with this diagnosis feel blamed, scapegoated and isolated, Rosie's workbook is a breath of fresh air. It does more than just provide information – it creates a space where you feel seen, heard and safe to explore your thoughts and feelings creatively.

From the very first page, Rosie's writing makes one thing clear: this book is not written *for* you, but *with* you. It is not a clinical manual, nor does it seek to 'fix' or water down the complexities of living with BPD. She does not write as a cold expert who talks down to you, but as a fellow traveller. Her words are grounded in her own lived experience, combined with deep compassion and an unflinching dedication to truth. You can feel her care and respect for the reader, and her intention to sit alongside you.

Rosie skilfully blends her personal insight with current research in neuroscience and attachment theory, appropriately drawing on the work of prominent figures in the field, such as Marsha Linehan, Anthony

Bateman and Peter Fonagy. While rigorous, the theories are never presented in a distant or clinical way. She brings them to life by making them deeply relatable and directly applicable to everyday experiences.

I particularly value how Rosie tackles the often-debated nature of the BPD diagnosis itself. Clearly, she does not shy away from difficult truths, like how diagnoses can be biased against women and marginalized communities, or how clinical approaches sometimes miss the bigger picture of social and cultural impacts on mental health. She reminds us that the label of BPD does not point to personal failure but instead reflects systemic ignorance, institutional shortcomings and epistemic injustice. Rosie's message is clear: living with BPD does not mean you are broken. If anything, it simply means you are navigating a world not always equipped for the depth and intensity of your emotions.

Another thing that strikes me is that the book touches on the overlap between BPD and neurodivergent traits. This is an area receiving more attention, but few resources explore it with such care and sensitivity. Rosie points out, for instance, how autistic girls and women can be misdiagnosed with BPD because their neurodivergent traits are mistaken for emotional dysregulation. She is clearly tuned into these crucial conversations and shines a much-needed light on subjects that are too often overlooked.

It is through the journal prompts that this workbook comes alive as a partner in self-discovery. These are not generic exercises; they are thoughtfully crafted to meet you where you are and allow you to explore challenging subjects at your own pace. For instance, the weekly emotion tracker does not simply ask for a 1–10 rating; it encourages you to identify specific emotions like sadness, joy, love or shame. This is especially helpful for those who feel things intensely but find it hard to put words to their emotions, a common BPD experience that can lead one to feel empty on the inside or frustrated and misunderstood in relationships. Rosie clearly understands these challenges and has designed activities that hit the mark.

By the time the reader reaches the final page, they may find that they have created something deeply personal and meaningful: a guided memoir or an autobiography of their emotions, patterns and relationships. It becomes something akin to a handbook, entirely unique to them, that can serve as a trusted companion during their most challenging times.

In a time defined by misinformation, political division and social tension, this book is a rare and much-needed offering. Thoughtful, compassionate and deeply human, Rosie Cappuccino's writing is filled with hope. And this is not the superficial kind of hope you sometimes find in self-help books. It is a real, grounded hope – one that acknowledges the pain and loneliness that can come with healing, while also celebrating the incredible resilience you can find within yourself to heal and thrive.

Imi Lo, mental health consultant and author
of *Emotional Sensitivity and Intensity*

Acknowledgments

Although I'm still the same person now as I was when I wrote my first book, my mind and heart have expanded in directions I didn't even know existed. Since then, I've married my husband, had a baby, developed my work as a teacher, grown friendships old and new... and written this book. Everything I wrote in the acknowledgments to my first book remains true and I continue to be grateful to everyone I thanked then. However, I would like to take this moment here to thank a few key people, either again or for the first time.

First, the readers of my blog and the first book. It's my privilege that you share parts of your lives with me, often aspects that feel painful, uncertain or difficult to share. I also appreciate the generous words of support and encouragement that so many of you send to me. Second, I want to thank Jane Evans, my editor at JKP for her brilliant guidance and for recognizing the value of non-stigmatizing books written by people with lived experience. Thank you to Laura Savage, Sarah Thomson and the entire team at JKP who helped bring this book to fruition.

I'm lucky to have many wonderful friends who helped me find enough confidence to be vulnerable all over again with another book. The reflective and exploratory nature of this second book prompted a lot of self-reflection and questions about my identity. Themes such as honesty, trust, safety, authenticity, connection and the complexities of language played out more than I ever predicted they would in the context of my friendships.

Astrid, for your consistent insights and affectionate honesty in this special friendship. Frances, for your priceless empathy, wisdom and humour. Sabina, for continually inspiring me and reminding me that my voice matters. Jonny, for thought-provoking conversations which helped me feel more comfortable in my own skin. Miss M., for always reminding me to 'be myself'. Finally, Kathryn, from *My Illustrated Mind*, for a beautiful, unique friendship. You know my emotions and thoughts from the inside out without my having to explain. I don't know how to thank you enough for everything you give me.

I also wanted to thank a few more people. Colleagues at work, your acceptance meant so much when I dared to open up more about my life. The numerous people who took care of my daughter to allow me time to write – I'm so grateful, and this book would not have been written without your caregiving.

Aya, my life-changing, life-affirming DBT therapist, for helping me out of what felt like chaos several years ago, transforming my relationship with my emotions and with myself when both of these felt bleak and raw. I still live by what you taught me. The way we conversed as equals, with humour and warmth, are tangible memories I invoke whenever I struggle today.

Finally, the biggest thank you of all is for my husband, Maciek. For everything – especially the happiness, humour and the light you brought to my life.

Introduction

I was on my way home from meeting a friend when I started sobbing in the middle of the street. Five minutes earlier, I'd been feeling buoyant, full of life. Now I felt such emptiness and despair that my thoughts had careered off down dark alleys... I was thinking about ending my life. Across the street there was a hospital, Accident & Emergency sign glowing red. I felt too frantic to travel home and, not knowing what else to do, I headed inside.

Instances like these happened frequently for a number of years. Once, a friend didn't reply to a message, and I panicked about why they weren't responding. My anxiety shifted to paranoia; I ran into the street at night without even knowing where I was going. Did everyone I love secretly hate me? And had I run outside because I was on the run from the police? It sounds extreme, but this is how it was for me. Outside a quiet corner shop, I managed to ground myself and walk home.

Another time, I was in the university library finalizing my dissertation when I became distressed. I called the number I'd been told to phone when I was in crisis. 'You have nothing to be suicidal about', the support worker at the end of the line told me. 'You have family, friends, an education, a job...'

The guilt of 'having it all' and still struggling was lacerating. Even the people trained to understand didn't understand. Why did everything hurt? What was wrong with me? Why couldn't I cope like everyone else?

☆ What is BPD?

BPD is a frightening and confusing mental health condition to experience. It is characterized by intense and painful emotions, quickly shifting moods, powerful urges to act on impulse and, often, an all-consuming anxiety about relationships. People with BPD may spiral into distress over events or interactions that seem insignificant to others. Individuals can experience terrifying thoughts about being worthless, disgusting or unlovable.

They may experience vast surges of anxiety, shame, anger or other emotions. During these heightened emotional states, individuals might be fearful of being abandoned or rejected by people important to them. They might make hasty decisions that are attempts to stop the pain in the short term, but that have long-term detrimental effects on health, relationships, careers, and so on.

Often, the emotional agony can feel so unbearable that individuals feel hollow or disconnected from themselves, their thoughts, others or the world in general. They might experience – temporarily – narratives in their mind representing their fears. These narratives are often related to relationships: *They have left me. Nobody really loves me. They are laughing at me behind my back.* Thinking about, or engaging in, self-harm and suicide is associated with this type of emotional distress. If you relate to these descriptions, you will know how agonizing this is – and how isolating it can feel.

The *Diagnostic and Statistical Manual of Mental Disorders 5-TR* (DSM-5-TR), published by the American Psychiatric Association, outlines nine criteria associated with BPD. For a diagnosis of BPD, individuals must, according to this influential publication, meet at least five of these nine criteria, experiencing them across various aspects of their life (such as family, work, study, friendships, romantic relationships). These must have been present since early adulthood (APA 2022).

The DSM-5-TR describes BPD as being distinguished by widespread changes in how a person feels, relates to others and thinks about themselves, combined with urges to act on impulse. The nine criteria it sets out include:

☆ Panic-stricken attempts to avoid being abandoned or rejected.

☆ Up-and-down relationships and oscillating between seeing a person as 'all good' or 'all bad'.

☆ A sense of self, values or identity that changes frequently and/or suddenly.

☆ Acting on impulse in ways that ultimately make life more challenging.

☆ Thinking about, or doing things related to, ending your life or injuring yourself.

☆ Emotions and moods that change quickly, for example feeling upset with life, on edge or anxious before feeling okay again a little while later.

☆ A long-term feeling of being empty or hollow.

☆ Feeling intensely angry and struggling to manage anger.

☆ Brief episodes of paranoia (feeling suspicious or somehow endangered even when there is no evidence of threat) during times of stress or experiencing dissociation (feeling disconnected from yourself, others or the world around you).

☆ Common experiences associated with BPD

When I was first diagnosed with BPD, I found it hard to relate to the criteria, even though I met most (if not all) of them. To help with understanding what the criteria might look across different contexts, here are some examples.

Panic-stricken attempts to avoid being abandoned or rejected

This relates to terror about being someone pushed away or left, even when this is unlikely. Individuals may act in anxious or distressed ways to try to stop their fears from becoming reality, such as repeatedly messaging to 'check the temperature' of a relationship or asking repeatedly for reassurance about how someone feels about them.

Separations, even temporary ones, may be really challenging, such as becoming upset after saying goodbye to a friend or feeling unable to cope when someone important goes on holiday. This criterion does not include suicidal or self-harm-related behaviours.

Do you relate to this? What does this look like for you in your life?

. . . .

. . . .

. . . .

. . . .

. . . .

. . . .

. . . .

Up-and-down relationships and oscillating between seeing a person as 'all good' or 'all bad'

Relationships of all kinds may feel peaceful one moment and scary the next. They may be fraught with anxiety and doubt ('Do they like me? Are they upset with me?'). It can be easy to feel close one moment and disconnected the next. At times, it can be challenging to hold on to the idea that people are a blend of positives and negatives, neither 'all good' or 'all bad'.

Does any of this resonate with you? In what way?

. . . .

. . . .

. . . .

. . . .

. . . .

. . . .

. . . .

A sense of self, values or identity that changes frequently and/or suddenly

An aspect of your identity, your values or priorities might shift and change. Your self-esteem might also fluctuate intensely, for example from feeling good about yourself in the morning to feeling worthless in the afternoon.

Sometimes, people might be social chameleons, taking on the characteristics of different groups to fit in, or they may start things and then change their mind about wanting to do them. All of this can make life unsettling and confusing.

Is any of this true for you? How does this show up in your life?

. . . .

. . . .

. . . .

. . . .

. . . .

. . . .

. . . .

. . . .

Acting on impulse in ways that ultimately make life more challenging

This relates to doing things that damage aspects of your life, such as your health, relationships or career, without stopping to think through the consequences. Examples could be quitting your course after getting lower than expected marks in an assignment or sending an angry message to a friend because they didn't reply to your messages.

Acting on impulse is often a response to strong emotions, but of course it can hurt both you and others. Note that this category does not include suicidal or self-harm-related behaviour.

Is this something which plays out in your life, and if so, how?

....

....

....

....

....

....

....

....

Thinking about, or doing things related to, ending your life or injuring yourself

This concerns suicide and self-harm; thinking about ending your life, planning or attempting suicide, as well as inflicting pain on yourself or injuring your body. As Chapter 3 explores, there are many reasons why someone might consider suicide or self-harm, and, if possible, it's important to be non-judgemental towards yourself if you're struggling with either (or both) of these.

Do you think about, or do, things related to ending your life or injuring yourself? Feel free to write it down, if you feel comfortable with this.

....

....

....

....

....

....

....

Emotions and moods that change quickly

You may have emotions and moods that feel very intense, all-consuming and even physically painful. Perhaps this is high levels of anxiety or irritability, extreme sadness or despair, strong anger or elation that feels 'too much'.

These emotional states tend to change quickly, perhaps over the course of a few minutes, hours or sometimes a day. These shifts in emotion and mood occur in response to events and experiences – often things that happen in relationships and social contexts. For example, you might go to bed feeling immense shame and distress because a friend hasn't replied to your message and then feel a surge of joy and relief when they reply the next morning.

Does any of this resonate for you and, if so, how?

. . . .

. . . .

. . . .

. . . .

. . . .

. . . .

. . . .

. . . .

A long-term feeling of being empty or hollow

This might be a deep-down feeling, similar to despair, hopelessness or dread. Some people describe it as a pit in their stomach, a void inside themselves or like being an empty shell. This long-term feeling can make a person feel numb or make life feel desolate. When positive feelings or experiences arise, it can be hard to hold on to them against such a bleak backdrop.

Is this something you feel and how would you describe it?

. . . .

. . . .

. . . .

. . . .

. . . .

. . . .

. . . .

. . . .

Feeling intensely angry and struggling to manage anger

High levels of anger that feel unmanageable; not knowing how to cope with this and it causing problems for you and for others. Such anger may seem out of proportion to the situation; however, it might be a response to feeling rejected, abandoned or invalidated by someone. Commonly, the emotion underneath anger is fear.

Do you struggle with anger? How does it affect you and others around you?

. . . .

. . . .

. . . .

. . . .

. . . .

. . . .

. . . .

Brief episodes of paranoia during times of stress or experiencing dissociation

Paranoia is when someone thinks they are under threat or feels in danger when there is no concrete reason to think that way. Examples include thinking that people are speaking negatively about you or plotting against you, when there is no or little evidence of this, or reading negativity into body language or messages when there is no ill-feeling there.

Dissociation describes feeling disconnected from yourself, others or the world. There are several types of dissociation, and they vary between individuals. Examples might be feeling like you're observing your life rather than living it, floating above your body or that you're looking at the world from behind glass. Sometimes it might involve gaps in your memory or not being sure of how you arrived somewhere.

For people with BPD, paranoia and dissociation tend to be brief, during times of intense stress. They can be frightening experiences for some people.

Have you experienced paranoia and/or dissociation and how does it feel for you?

. . . .

. . . .

. . . .

. . . .

. . . .

. . . .

. . . .

. . . .

☆ What do my difficulties look like?

Being sensitive to rejection and a fear of abandonment are key struggles for me. I experience intense emotions which are liable to colour my thoughts and my perspective on myself, others and my life. When I'm happy, I tend to feel positive about myself, others and life. When I'm upset, I often feel critical towards myself, feel disconnected from others and find it hard to feel loved. I have also spent many years struggling with self-harm and feeling suicidal.

During moments of panic, I can become frantic and experience paranoia; I can think that a frightening situation is happening, even when it's not. When I was younger I had strong feelings of anger too. I felt like I would explode with rage. I also used to feel hollow sometimes, as if I felt homesick for a place that didn't exist.

Everyone who gets diagnosed with BPD has their own personality, life circumstances and personal history. Whilst every person with a BPD diagnosis is different, common themes emerge.

Is there anything else you wanted to note down about your experience?

. . . .

. . . .

. . . .

. . . .

. . . .

. . . .

. . . .

. . . .

. . . .

☆ Why do I struggle so much?

It's understandable to be curious about origins or causes of your difficulties. I used to ask myself questions like 'Why me?', 'What is the cause of this?' and 'Was I born this way?'. Perhaps you have any questions of your own that you would like to note.

....

....

....

....

....

....

....

....

Answering questions about origins or causes of what is known as BPD is complex (as it is for many mental health diagnoses). First, there is no single identifiable cause of BPD. Second, how a person develops BPD is contested – so too is the diagnostic category itself, as I will explore later in this book. Whilst more studies seem to be needed, including into the neurobiology of people with this diagnosis, researchers have identified several possible factors that may interact with one another leading a person to develop what is known as BPD.

Difficult or traumatic experiences as a child or young person

It's common for people diagnosed with BPD to have experienced difficult or traumatic experiences as a child or young person. In fact, a 2019 study by the University of Manchester reported that more than 70 per cent of people with a diagnosis of BPD reported having at least one traumatic experience during childhood (Porter et al. 2020). The study also found that people with BPD were 13 times more likely to report having experienced childhood trauma than people without mental health problems.

It's hard to define what makes an experience particularly difficult or traumatic for a child or young person. However, they might best be described as events or experiences which were difficult for a child or young person to cope with, and which made them feel scared, unsafe, unsupported, trapped or powerless. These events or experiences may have involved abuse or neglect. They may have been one-off or repeated, and they could have happened anywhere: home, school, in the community or elsewhere.

Difficult or traumatic experiences are so varied they are hard to list. However, the following are possible examples:

☆ feeling isolated, different, lonely or unsupported
☆ having a family member with an illness or difficulty that made your life difficult
☆ losing someone important or special (as a result of a bereavement or for another reason)
☆ having difficulties with your emotions, including not understanding them or how to handle them
☆ having nobody who understands your feelings, your way of thinking or seeing the world
☆ being rejected or abandoned in some way
☆ being bullied, made to feel inferior or that you don't belong
☆ experiencing mental, physical, sexual abuse or neglect.

Perhaps you experienced difficult or traumatic events as a child or young person; maybe these are still ongoing. Feel free to note down your experiences here, if it feels okay to write them down.

....

....

....

....

....

....

As everyone experiences events in different ways and has unique life circumstances, what one person might find difficult or traumatic another person might not. It's up to each individual to choose what they define as 'difficult' or 'traumatic'. There's no scale to rate one person's struggle as more or less worthy of understanding and of being taken seriously. If something hurt, it hurt. Your feelings mattered then, and they matter now.

TRYING TO STOP FURTHER PAIN

Individuals who have experienced difficult or traumatic events might try hard to stop themselves from experiencing further pain. This might be with specific ways of responding to the world, relating to other people or themselves. A few years ago, one of my friendships ended abruptly, and I felt devastated. I started looking for signs of rejection in other friendships, even when there was no rejection there. I replayed conversations in my mind and reread messages; every interaction made me feel vulnerable, and I was scared to trust. I asked for lots of reassurance in an attempt to protect myself, but this made me more anxious and upset.

Do you have any patterns of thinking or things you do which may relate to difficult or traumatic experiences? Here's space to note them down.

Invalidating environments

Dr Marsha M. Linehan, Professor of Psychology and Adjunct Professor of Psychiatry and Behavioral Sciences at the University of Washington, famously created one of the most well-known treatments for people with BPD: dialectical behaviour therapy (DBT). DBT recognizes the role that an 'invalidating environment' can play in the development of BPD, especially for individuals who are naturally more sensitive to feeling their emotions intensely.

Dr Linehan described an 'invalidating environment' as one in which 'the communication of private experiences is met by erratic, inappropriate, and extreme responses' (Linehan 1993, p.49). In other words, an 'invalidating environment' teaches a child that it's wrong, shameful or bad to have – and share – their emotions or feelings. It's an environment that dismisses or shames a child for expressing how they feel or what's important to them. It could involve children:

☆ Being shamed for the intensity of their emotions or for being sensitive to things that others may not feel: 'You're making a fuss over nothing.' 'Drama-queen!' 'Why do you have to be so sensitive?' 'Grow a thicker skin.'

☆ Being told, directly or indirectly, to hide their emotions or avoid expressing what's important to them: 'Stop crying!' 'Wipe that smile off your face.' 'Don't do that when you're under my roof.'

☆ Not being taken seriously or believed when they share how they feel or what's important to them: 'Those are crocodile tears.' 'It's not a big deal.' 'I don't think you're scared really.'

An invalidating environment could be at home, school, in the community or a combination of places. Invalidating environments may be created knowingly; for example, when adults deliberately show children that their feelings and views don't matter. They may also be created unintentionally; for example, through adults' lack of awareness of their actions or discomfort with seeing others expressing themselves.

Growing up in an invalidating environment doesn't mean a child will always go on to develop struggles with emotional regulation and related difficulties. Dr Linehan theorized that it's an invalidating environment combined with an individual's innate emotional sensitivity that leads to the kinds of difficulties associated with a BPD diagnosis. Whether they contribute to a child developing serious mental health difficulties or not, invalidating environments reduce opportunities for children to learn how to regulate their emotions and relate positively to themselves.

After years of being feeling unseen and misunderstood, some children may grow into adults longing to be seen and understood. Others may be adults who believe their feelings and opinions don't matter at all. If you relate to the concept of invalidating environments, take some time to write about your experiences. How did it feel to be in this kind of environment and how do you think it affected you?

. . . .

. . . .

. . . .

. . . .

. . . .

. . . .

. . . .

. . . .

. . . .

Insecure attachments and hypersensitivity

Attachment theory explains how an infant's bond with their caregivers shapes their emotional development, how they view themselves and experience future relationships. A growing body of research theorizes an association between BPD and insecure attachment, specifically insecure attachment involving a longing for closeness mixed with anxiety – especially, anxiety about becoming dependent on or being rejected by someone close (Agrawal et al. 2004).

Dr John G. Gunderson, who was Professor of Psychiatry at Harvard Medical School, recognized that descriptions of insecure attachment are similar to the responses of people with BPD when they are struggling. These responses include seeking help and connection from an attachment figure, so-called 'clinging' (not my preferred word) and trying to gauge the emotional closeness within the relationship, as well as anxieties about relying on this person for support. As Peter Fonagy, training and supervising analyst at the British Psychoanalytical Society and Professor of Contemporary Psychoanalysis and Developmental Science at University College London, explains: people with BPD are 'exquisitely sensitive to all interpersonal interactions' and usually have 'hypersensitive attachment systems within interpersonal contexts' (Bateman and Fonagy 2010, p.12).

This is a great description of me. Over the years, I've noticed my capacity to feel very strong emotional connections with certain people. My moods are often contingent on how these people respond to me and how connected I feel to them at any given moment. My connection with these people is like an invisible thread. If these people reciprocate emotionally to me, are responsive and show warmth, the thread between us feels strong and taut; I feel safe, positive about myself and life. If these people are unresponsive to me, seem distant or cold, the thread between us feels weak and loose; I feel anxious, my mood drops, and my self-esteem shrinks. These people don't intend to exert such an influence on me and may not even be aware of it. Nonetheless, they unintentionally hold huge sway over how I feel about myself and my life.

Do you relate to any of this? If the invisible threads between you and significant others feel strong, how do you feel? If they feel weak, how do you feel?

. . . .

. . . .

. . . .

. . . .

As I will share throughout this book, I've learnt how to become less reactive to these relational shifts over the years. I panic less frequently than before when friends don't reply to my messages. I spend less time replaying conversations in my mind and imagining how my words were interpreted by others. I manage conflicts and moments of disconnection more effectively than before.

I've never sought to fully erase my emotional response to relational shifts though. I'm human, a relational being who wants – and needs – to be emotionally responsive within my relationships. Emotional connections are surely one of the richest sources of contentment and fulfilment in most people's lives. I feel intensely in relation to the people I love. I would never want to remove that completely. Writing about this makes me feel exposed; however, as I will share later, it's at the heart of who I am and is, undeniably, a strength. Like me, do you feel that your emotional connections with others are at the core of who you are too? Feel free to write a little about this, if you would like to.

. . . .

. . . .

. . . .

. . . .

. . . .

. . . .

. . . .

. . . .

☆ A contentious diagnosis

Just mention BPD in a room of mental health professionals and sparks will fly. The concept of BPD as a diagnostic category elicits strong debate – for good reason. A diagnosis like BPD is not just a note on someone's medical records. A diagnosis, especially one as stigmatized as BPD, has a real-world impact on an individual's access to care, how others relate to them – including people in positions of power such as health, social care and education professionals – and, for some people, their identity and livelihood.

I knew this diagnosis was contentious when I received it, but I embraced it regardless. I needed a name to constellate my experiences, an atlas to navigate these confusing and frightening experiences. My feelings about my diagnosis are complicated, but I choose to embrace it – even though I sometimes feel guilt. Let me now share some of the reasons why the diagnosis is so contentious.

Contention #1: Natural responses to difficult life experiences or trauma should not be defined as 'personality disorder'

Some people argue that it's unfair and unethical to label people experiencing understandable responses to trauma as having a 'personality disorder'. They argue that the diagnosis is dehumanizing and akin to telling them that there's something disordered – wrong – with their personality. As the word personality is quasi-synonymous with the essence of who we are, the diagnosis can feel like a character slur, an indictment of being damaged at the core.

I don't understand the term personality disorder to mean I'm defective. I look to the definition of 'personality' as it's often used in psychology – to refer to patterns of thinking, feeling, responding and relating to others and the world. I don't see my personality and having borderline personality disorder as being one and the same: I am so much more than my BPD. I have had difficult experiences but feel these can still be understood alongside having a BPD diagnosis. That being said, the words 'personality' and 'disorder' made me scared to speak about my diagnosis for years, and I believe renaming this diagnosis would be helpful.

Contention #2: The diagnosis blames individuals and erases accountability

Some people believe that the BPD diagnosis positions an individual as the problem, rather than the people who have inflicted harm or the systems that perpetuated this. Some state that the diagnosis waives responsibility and erases accountability from the people or systems causing damage, scapegoating the diagnosed individual and causing further trauma. Many describe the BPD diagnosis as legitimizing – and perpetuating –abuse, neglect, inequality and violence of various kinds.

These are valid concerns. I've experienced professionals who are able to see my diagnosis and acknowledge the harms I've experienced, without blaming me for them. I don't believe that diagnosing someone with BPD makes a person unable to call out harm. In my opinion, a lack of empathy, understanding and critical thinking is what prevents that.

Contention #3: The BPD diagnosis harms women

According to the DSM-5-TR, approximately 75 per cent of people diagnosed with BPD are female. Numerous individuals and groups believe that the BPD diagnosis is particularly harmful to women and LGBTQ+ people. Many academics and activists have expressed that this diagnosis pathologizes, and punishes, women for entirely valid responses to injustice, oppression or abuse, including sexual abuse or sexual violence. In 'Women at the margins: A critique of the diagnosis of borderline personality disorder' Clare Shaw and Gillian Proctor write that the diagnosis of BPD has a 'fundamental failure to locate and understand distress within its social context'. They also situate the BPD label within a wider historical narrative, referencing the diagnosis of 'hysteria', often given to discredit experiences of sexual abuse, and accusations of witchcraft (Shaw and Proctor 2005).

In 'The new hysteria: Borderline personality disorder and epistemic injustice', Dorfman and Reynolds (2023) argue that the diagnostic criteria of BPD pathologizes female expressions of sexuality, impulsivity and anger. They write that 'the diagnosis of BPD places women in a double bind in which they are punished for both conforming to and breaking away from societal stereotypes' (p.166). Sometimes, it feels like women experiencing immense distress as a result of painful experiences – including some that may be ongoing – cannot win. Too 'quiet' and they don't get seen. Too 'loud' and they get discredited.

There is also a growing awareness that numerous neurodivergent girls and women are being misdiagnosed with BPD when they are in fact autistic and/or have ADHD. Being diagnosed with BPD when you are actually autistic or have ADHD (or both) can be, as many individuals attest, deeply invalidating, painful and traumatic. Whilst there are some points in common between people with BPD and autistic people and/or those with ADHD (such as high levels of anxiety, becoming overwhelmed at times or using masking as a way of coping with social situations), they are very distinct diagnoses and sets of experiences which cannot, and should not, be conflated.

Contention #4: The BPD diagnosis harms LGBTQ+ people, including trans people

There is increasing research that LGBTQ+ people, including trans people, seem to be overrepresented amongst those diagnosed with BPD. It worries me that people may have their sexuality and/or gender unnecessarily, and unfairly, pathologized by professionals, along with any adverse experiences that they may have experienced as a result of prejudice or stigma on this basis too.

In their article 'Is there a bias in the diagnosis of borderline personality disorder among lesbian, gay, and bisexual patients?', Rodriguez-Seijas, Morgan and Zimmerman (2021) suggest that 'clinicians may be predisposed to provide a BPD diagnosis to sexual minority patients'. They found that the 'diagnostic disparity was highest for bisexual compared with heterosexual patients'. In 'Male homosexuality and borderline personality disorder: A review', Cavale, Chand Singh and Hemchand (2024) describe the pathologization and harmful attitudes faced by gay and bisexual men in mental health settings (which echo those faced by women mentioned in the section above).

Trans people also seem to be more likely to be diagnosed with BPD – and unjustly pathologized for being transgender. In 'My personality is not disordered and neither is my gender. Response to: Evaluation of

personality disorders in patients with gender identity disorder (GID)',
Porter, Smith and Watts (2023) write that 'pathologising transgender
identities indicates a viewpoint that this is not a natural and beautiful experience, but a condition which could – and perhaps should – be
cured'. I'm strongly against all conversion practices – 'interventions that
seek to change, cure, or suppress an individual's sexual orientation or
gender identity'– and hope to see laws passed in the UK and beyond to
prevent these harmful practices (see Stonewall 2025).

I've noticed over the years that lots of my blog and book readers are
LGBTQ+. Your experiences and identities are valid and deserve nothing
less than full respect and equality. I know that not every person who is
LGBTQ+ faces struggles with their emotional wellbeing, but I know that
many do in some way. As Dr Brendan J. Dunlop (2022) writes: '[A] felt
sense, even from a very young age, that you do not fit in can be incredibly
difficult'. His book *The Queer Mental Health Workbook: A Creative Self-Help
Guide Using CBT, CFT and DBT* is a brilliant resource.

Contention #5: The BPD diagnosis doesn't stand up to scientific scrutiny

Some argue that the BPD diagnosis doesn't stand up to scientific scru-
tiny. Mulder and Tyrer (2023) write that BPD has 'a complete lack of
specificity' and is a 'spurious condition unsupported by science'. They,
along with other researchers, note that the features of BPD overlap with
'almost every other psychiatric disorder, particularly ADHD, bipolar disorder and other mood disorders'. Consequently, there have been calls to
remove the category of BPD from medical classification systems, such as
the International Classification of Diseases Tenth and Eleventh Revisions
(ICD10 and ICD11).

Contention #6: The BPD diagnosis results in negative attitudes and being treated harshly

In their study on 'difficult patients', Koekkoek, van Meijel and Hutschemaekers (2006) found that individuals with a diagnosis of BPD were
judged more negatively by staff than patients with other diagnoses such
as schizophrenia even when they presented in the same way. Too often,

people with this diagnosis are coded as drama-queens, attention-seekers and manipulators. Their distress is deemed childish, or even performative, not something to be taken seriously or to be supported. Dr Jay Watts, Consultant Psychotherapist, Honorary Senior Lecturer and journalist (2016) writes that individuals diagnosed with BPD are positioned as 'too sexual, too clever and too aware of their actions to deserve care, interest and respect'.

In 'Structural stigma and its impact on healthcare for borderline personality disorder: A scoping review', Klein, Fairweather and Lawn (2022) write that those with 'a diagnosis of BPD and their carers/ families are often confronted with structural stigma when accessing health services for their mental health condition'. They note that individuals with BPD 'consistently report receiving suboptimal levels of care from health services including not being believed or dismissed in relation to the nature and severity of their presentation'. Similarly, in an article on 'difficult patient' status, Sandra H. Sulzer (2015) writes that her findings 'suggest patients with BPD are routinely labelled "difficult", and subsequently routed out of care through a variety of direct and indirect means'. I think many people with this diagnosis will recognize this struggle to be taken seriously and offered effective and compassionate care.

How do you feel about the BPD diagnosis?

Some people argue that the BPD diagnosis should be abolished and replaced with different ways of conceptualizing emotional distress. The Power Threat Meaning Framework, for example, 'is an overarching structure for identifying patterns in emotional distress, unusual experiences and troubling behaviour, as an alternative to psychiatric diagnosis and classification' (Johnstone and Boyle 2018). Others argue that we should keep the diagnosis but disrupt the negative attitudes and dismantle the structural stigma.

Do any of the contentions described above resonate for you? Do you think the diagnosis is helpful, harmful or perhaps a mix of the two? How you feel about this diagnosis is completely up to you; and if you're not sure, it's okay not to know. The important thing is that your thoughts matter – here's space to write them down.

. . . .

. . . .

. . . .

. . . .

. . . .

. . . .

. . . .

. . . .

☆ This book is for you

This book is for anyone who struggles to regulate intense and quickly changing emotions, especially within relationships – whether romantic, friendships, family, at work, and so on. You don't need a formal diagnosis of BPD to use this book. I've tried hard to make sure this book welcomes everyone regardless of their stance on how helpful or harmful BPD is as a diagnostic category.

This book contains spaces for you to write and draw, but please try not to think about whether your writing or drawing is 'good'. This book is not about 'good' or 'bad' writing or drawing; it's about expression and exploration. You also don't have to share what you write or draw with anyone – although you can of course if you want to. For most people, this book will be most effective when worked through in order. Take it at your own pace. The reflections and creative prompts might prompt strong emotions – and that's okay. However, if anything ever feels too painful, take a break and ask for support if you feel able and if this would be helpful. There are support organizations listed in the 'Support and Resources' section at the back of this book.

Writing this book has clarified my thinking and strengthened my identity as a person with this highly stigmatized diagnosis. I feel more fully 'myself' than I did when I started out writing it. I hope this book makes you feel understood, helps you feel supported and brings you the warmth you may not always feel when you're distressed. Why not take a moment to write down three things you hope to get from this book?

1. . . . .

. . . .

2. . . . .

. . . .

3. . . . .

. . . .

CHAPTER 1

Understanding Myself
(Even When I Confuse Myself)

In some ways, I've always known myself well. Even as a child I knew how I wanted to spend my time, what was important to me and the kind of person I wanted to be. I was an introspective, imaginative and thoughtful child who read a lot of books and wrote stories, poems and journals. These things were, and still are, my way of making sense of myself and the world around me. In other ways, though, I grew up feeling painfully confused about my emotions and unsettled about my identity as a person who feels a lot and thinks a lot. I asked myself many questions like: *Are my emotions real? Is it even possible to feel like this? Does anyone else feel like this? Will anyone even believe me?* I struggled to pull the threads of myself into coherent narratives that, first, felt believable (to myself and to others) and, second, felt comfortable.

Over the last few years, though, with the help of people I've met along the way, I've untangled these threads of my life and woven them together. I know they're all real, and, most of the time, I appreciate each of their colours. I really hope this chapter helps you begin to unravel those aspects of yourself that may feel, at times, tricky or confusing.

☆ Quickly changing emotions

When I was younger, a psychiatrist I was seeing gave me a mood diary to complete. She asked me to rate my mood from 1 to 10 each day so we could observe patterns. Whilst I had overall moods that were lower or higher, my emotions could shift many times per day. I could shift from suicidal in the morning, to panicky at lunchtime, to euphoric in the evening and back to despair at bedtime. How could I capture that with a daily rating? I told the psychiatrist that tracking my moods in this way would not show my reality. She told me to write an average score for each day, and, after a couple of weeks, I had a flat line right across the middle of the grid. My quickly changing highs and lows were rendered invisible and, yet again, I felt unseen.

Do you experience quickly changing emotions and what are they like for you?

. . . .

. . . .

. . . .

. . . .

. . . .

. . . .

. . . .

Your emotions are real

It's not easy to feel many different emotions, often intensely, in quick succession. It can be painful, confusing or even frightening. It can be hard for the individual, and sometimes others, to trust that how they are feeling is genuine. When the psychiatrist didn't acknowledge my rapid shifts in emotion, I doubted their reality: *Am I really happy when I felt suicidal this morning? If I felt suicidal last night, how can I be happy now?*

Do you ever doubt the genuineness of your emotions? And has any-one ever said or done anything to make you doubt how you're feeling?

. . . .

. . . .

. . . .

. . . .

. . . .

. . . .

. . . .

. . . .

It took me many years to fully accept that emotions aren't any less genuine because they change quickly. No matter how long emotions last, they deserve to be acknowledged. Sadness that lasts a month isn't less legitimate than sadness that lasts an hour. A moment of joy isn't less real than a week of happiness. To have emotions that change fast doesn't mean you are dramatizing or faking them.

Here are some affirmations for acknowledging quickly changing emotions as genuine, with some space for your own. Write them down somewhere you can see them or repeat them to yourself throughout the day.

My emotions are real, no matter how often they come and go.

My emotions are genuine, regardless of how long they last.

My emotions are free to appear and disappear as they wish.

I am allowed to feel . . . . for as long as I need.

. . . .

. . . .

. . . .

. . . .

. . . .

☆ Intense emotions

For most people with BPD, it's not just the speed and frequency at which emotions change that is challenging, it's also their intensity. Emotions can feel dialled up to full volume. They can hit the body with full force, reverberating through every vein, bone and pore. They seem to permeate thoughts, colouring worldview and sense of self. A light wash of anxiety can be a soaring wave of panic; slight sadness can be a deluge of despair; and mild irritation can be rage.

Dr Marsha M. Linehan described that 'Borderline individuals are the psychological equivalent of third-degree-burn patients. They simply have, so to speak, no emotional skin. Even the slightest touch or movement can create immense suffering' (cited in Cloud 2009). This quotation, or a variation of it, is often shared amongst people with BPD probably because it evokes the visceral pain that many people with BPD feel when they experience intense emotions. A word or a glance can prompt an emotion that's felt like a surgeon's cut without anaesthetic; intense emotions can have a physical dimension to them. The strongest emotional pain I've ever experienced was far stronger than any physical pain I've ever felt. When I was preparing for the birth of my daughter, I wasn't scared of the pain. I believed that the emotional pain I'd experienced would outweigh any physical pain.

It's hard to convey the intensity of emotions to people who don't experience their emotions in this way. Over the years, though, I've experimented with analogies through drawing and creative writing to try to capture the intensity of emotions:

- ☆ drowning in emotion
- ☆ being electrocuted by emotion
- ☆ being strangled or suffocated by emotion
- ☆ being swallowed by a blue whale of sadness
- ☆ emotions like fire and ice.

Here's space to write your own analogies for intense and painful emotions. Like me, you may want to use words that invoke pain or power, such as fierce animals or forces of nature, or you may have ideas of your own. Alternatively, you may prefer to draw images and, if so, I've left space for you to do this below.

☆ Growing up feeling different

Since I was little, my emotions have been wild horses. When I cut my toe in a paddling pool, I cried for the rest of the afternoon. When I left primary (elementary) school and started secondary (high school), I cried in the toilets every day. I struggled with panic, anger and overwhelming sadness as a teenager. I used reading and creative writing as escapism, but sometimes the feelings got so big I couldn't imagine myself into other worlds away from them. After school, I would lie on the floor in private, panicking and crying, earthing myself like lightning striking a tree to discharge the current to the earth.

I hurt myself physically to help me survive surges of emotion and the shame that accompanied them. Afterwards, I would emerge from my bedroom, exhausted and embarrassed with puffy eyes ringed with red. I was ashamed and knew that I was upsetting the people who loved me. I was frustrated that no matter how hard I tried I couldn't be 'like everyone else' and 'control' my emotions.

I experienced suicidal thoughts on repeat for two reasons: shame and loneliness. No matter how hard I tried to be thoughtful and caring towards others, I felt like a monster for not being able to contain my anxiety, anger and sadness. Along with shame and loneliness, my other overriding emotion was confusion. How could I be hurting myself and feeling suicidal when I also had countless happy moments having fun with people I loved, and who loved me, and doing things that made me excited about life? There were two parts of me: one who loved life with her huge open heart, and one who found this huge open heart too painful for life.

Can you relate to any of my feelings growing up? What was it like for you to have quickly changing, intense emotions as a child and young person?

. . . .

. . . .

. . . .

. . . .

. . . .

. . . .

. . . .

. . . .

Some people feel emotions differently – and that's okay

DBT taught me to respond to my emotions in a new way. It also taught me that I didn't need to become someone else to live more easily. Whilst the other talking therapies that I'd tried before DBT helped me formulate new narratives about myself and my life, none of them had fully grasped my quickly changing intense emotions and how painful it felt to be alive.

My DBT therapist was the first professional – and the first person – who recognized the force of my emotions and how powerless I was in the face of them. Previous therapists told me to do things that others could manage, but I couldn't do. Before I share some of what she taught me, here are some reminders that it's okay to feel emotions differently. I've left some space for you to write some of your own reminders too.

I'm a person who feels emotions very intensely and that's okay.

I'm allowed to be sensitive to things.

It's okay to feel emotions deeply.

. . . .

. . . .

. . . .

. . . .

. . . .

. . . .

Perhaps you would like to make a poster with your own reminders. You could stick this up somewhere you'll see it every day or even take a photo of it and set it as your phone wallpaper.

☆ Understanding emotions
Emotions have functions

One of the first things I learnt in DBT was that emotions have functions. According to evolutionary psychology, human emotions have evolved over millennia to ensure the survival of the species. Emotions communicate key messages that tell us things about ourselves, others and our environment. Emotions also motivate us to act in certain ways. As a result, they are associated with physiological events, such as a change in heart rate, breathing, facial expression, and so on. Take fear, for example, which communicates a possible threat to ourselves or people we care about. It motivates us to keep ourselves or others safe; for example, running away, calling for help or trying to look less appealing to hurt. Associated physiological responses include an increased heart rate, tense muscles and reduced digestion – all efforts diverted to survival.

Until I started DBT, the idea that emotions have a function was abstract to me. I didn't relate the concept to myself and my life. However, acknowledging this idea within the context of my life meant I started to see my emotions as friends, not enemies. I began to explore what my emotions were communicating, even if their messages were coded or rooted in past experiences rather than in my present situation. I found grains of truth hidden within their layers – truths which needed, and deserved, to be recognized. It went something like this: *I texted a friend about something that means a lot to me, and they haven't replied. I feel the emotion of shame. I feel rejected and disconnected. Maybe I should be more careful with sharing my thoughts, so people don't think I'm 'difficult' and I end up alone.* Even though my shame was not warranted in this example – there is nothing wrong with wanting to talk about things that feel important – I could see the emotion was an attempt to keep me connected to others and that my feeling of disconnection felt very real.

In Table 1.1, I've summarized ten key emotions, what they tend to communicate and motivate us to do, as well as their associated physical responses. Of course, everyone is different, so variation in how these emotions are experienced is natural. I've therefore left space in the right-hand column for you to add your own notes about how you experience these emotions. Just as an aside, I think of guilt as occurring when I've broken my values and possibly hurt someone in the process and think of shame as happening when I've done something and predict this will result in social disapproval or rejection. I think of envy as a longing for something that someone else has; whereas jealousy is a fear of someone taking what you already have.

In Chapter 3, we will explore when to act in accordance with what an emotion is communicating and motivating us to do and when honouring an emotion's message in a different way might be more helpful. For more information on the functions of emotions, please see *DBT Skills Training Handouts and Worksheets* by Dr Marsha M. Linehan (2015).

Table 1.1 Ten key emotions

Emotion	What this emotion often motivates us to do, and physical responses often associated with it
Sadness	To seek comfort. To slow down. To rest. To yearn for the thing or person.
	Feeling tired or lethargic. Low energy. Moving slowly.
	. . . .
	. . . .
	. . . .
Anger	To push back against the feeling of threat or unfairness. To try to put things the way that feels 'right'.
	Heart racing. Feeling hot. Tense muscles. Urges to lash out verbally or physically.
	. . . .
	. . . .
	. . . .

cont.

Fear/Anxiety	To seek help or a sense of safety. To run away, avoid, hide, freeze.
	Heart racing. Shaking. Wide eyes. Vomiting and diarrhoea. Hypervigilance.
	. . . .
	. . . .
	. . . .
Happiness/Joy	To seek more of the feeling. To share the feeling.
	Laughing. Smiling. Moving fast. High energy.
	. . . .
	. . . .
	. . . .
Love	To seek more time and closeness with this person or doing this thing. To share the feeling.
	Feeling energetic, connected and good about yourself.
	. . . .
	. . . .
	. . . .
Guilt	To repair the damage done. To make up for wrongdoing.
	Looking at the floor. Feeling small. Feeling the urge to say sorry or make a change.
	. . . .
	. . . .
	. . . .
Shame	To hide the thing or part of oneself that feels immoral. To withdraw from others. To fear connection.
	Looking down or avoiding eye contact. Wanting to shrink or disappear.
	. . . .
	. . . .
	. . . .

Envy	To feel negative or spiteful towards people being envied. To feel motivated to change yourself and gain what you want.
	Physical tension or discomfort.
	. . . .
	. . . .
	. . . .
Jealousy	To want to remove competition. To want to keep hold of what you have so no one else can take it. To feel suspicious about a person or possessive of someone.
	Hypervigilance. Anxiety.
	. . . .
	. . . .
	. . . .
Disgust	To move away from the person whose values or ideas feel repulsive. To remove the thing which feels contaminating and get as far away from it as possible.
	Vomiting or feeling sick.
	. . . .
	. . . .
	. . . .

☆ Emotions trackers

I've created two emotion trackers: daily and weekly. You can use one of these or both of them together. I recommend filling them in for a couple of weeks before reflecting on what patterns and rhythms of emotion are playing out in your life. I have also created some prompts to help you do this below. More copies of these trackers are available for download and print at www.jkp.com/catalogue/book/9781805014096.

➜ DAILY TRACKER

Day: ....

Emotion intensity out of 10	Morning	Afternoon	Evening	Notes
Sadness				
Anger				
Fear/Anxiety				
Happiness/Joy				
Love				
Guilt				
Shame				
Envy				
Jealousy				
Disgust				

↗ WEEKLY TRACKER

Week beginning: ....

Emotion intensity out of 10*	Monday	Tuesday	Wednesday	Thursday	Friday	Saturday	Sunday	Notes
Sadness								
Anger								
Fear/Anxiety								
Happiness/Joy								
Love								
Guilt								
Shame								
Envy								
Jealousy								
Disgust								

*You experience multiple waves of the same emotion more than once in a day, so rate the emotion's intensity as many times as you need to.

Reflecting on patterns in your emotions

DAILY TRACKER

What have you noticed from tracking your emotions daily?

....

....

....

....

....

....

Are there times of day when you tend to feel a certain way?

....

....

....

....

....

....

Are there times of day that tend to be more or less challenging? For example, I often feel my happiest in the morning and lowest in the evening.

....

....

....

....

....

....

Note down any patterns that may be emerging in your trackers. In the next section, we will explore possible prompting events for emotions (interpersonal, routine and schedule, environmental and physical).

. . . .

. . . .

. . . .

. . . .

. . . .

. . . .

WEEKLY TRACKER
What have you noticed from tracking your emotions weekly?

. . . .

. . . .

. . . .

. . . .

. . . .

. . . .

Are there any days of the week when you tend to feel a certain way?

. . . .

. . . .

. . . .

. . . .

. . . .

. . . .

Are there days of the week that tend to be more or less challenging?

....

....

....

....

....

....

Note down any patterns that may be emerging from completing weekly trackers.

....

....

....

....

....

....

Further questions for reflection

Are there days or weeks across the month which feel more or less challenging than others? If you experience hormonal changes across the month, do you think these could be having an effect on your emotions?

....

....

....

....

....

....

Are there any months that feel more or less challenging? Some people find that certain anniversaries or traditions affect their emotions a lot.

. . . .

. . . .

. . . .

. . . .

. . . .

. . . .

Is there any seasonal variation in how you feel? And do your emotions tend to be affected by the weather?

. . . .

. . . .

. . . .

. . . .

. . . .

. . . .

☆ Prompting events for intense emotions

You may have noticed that certain events tend to spark off emotions. These events could be things that happen in your relationships, schedule or routine, environment or physical experiences like illness. Before DBT, I thought of my emotions as lightning bolts striking at random out of nowhere. My inner world was so chaotic that most of the time I didn't notice the events that were setting them in motion. I was too caught up in emotions to acknowledge where one emotion ended and the next one started.

When I did notice an event activating an emotion, I struggled to believe in the connection. The events seemed too small to prompt such a huge surge of emotion. I didn't know anyone else who experienced life with such a thin layer between themselves and the world. How could my phone lighting up with a message make me feel alive again? How could a minor health problem set off all-consuming panic? It felt impossible; like emptying an ocean with one cup or felling a forest with a single chop. Even if this were real, I wasn't sure I wanted it to be, in case it meant I was pathetic or, worse, disingenuous.

DBT taught me to notice the connection between my emotions and what was happening in my life. Conversations with others who felt similar to me via my blog and social media taught me that I wasn't the only person in the world to experience this. Over time, I noticed four types of events that prompted intense emotions: interpersonal, routine- and schedule-related and physical. Let's explore these now.

Interpersonal events

Things that happen in my relationships and in social situations are the most common prompts for my intense emotions. As mentioned in the Introduction, Professors Anthony Bateman and Peter Fonagy note that people with BPD are 'exquisitely sensitive to all interpersonal interactions' and usually have 'hypersensitive attachment systems within interpersonal contexts' (Bateman and Fonagy 2010, p.12). When I care about my relationship with someone, then my emotions and self-esteem can fluctuate based on how connected I feel to this person at any given moment.

Interpersonal events that set off intense emotions in me can be within romantic relationships, friendships, family, at work, and so on. However, these tend to happen most frequently with people close to me, individuals who have a significant role in my life or people in positions of power such as healthcare professionals or educators. If I like, respect or admire someone, especially if I value this person's presence in my life, then my emotions can be particularly reactive.

If I don't consciously relax around these people, I am hypervigilant. I startle easily and feel on edge. Words – spoken or written – facial expressions and body language push and pull on my emotions. If they walk towards me or my phone lights up with a message from them, I get a surge of anxiety. If I read the interaction as negative, I panic. *Did I upset them? Do they dislike me now? Will they cut me out of their life?* If it feels positive, I feel relief. Soon after my anxiety starts again. *Did I talk too much? Did I overwhelm them? Why are they not replying?*

By contrast, there are some people whom I admire and care about deeply but who don't prompt this emotional upheaval in me. Take my husband, for example. He has a calming influence on me and makes me feel more relaxed about life than anyone I've ever met. My ease within relationships is not related to how much I like or care about someone, though – some of the most fulfilling, meaningful and also enjoyable relationships in my life prompt anxiety in me at times. These people who set off anxiety in me don't intend to – quite the opposite actually. They also may be unaware of the anxiety I feel because I don't always feel able to tell them or may need time to build trust before telling them.

After many years of being confused about why some people set off anxiety in me and some don't, I'm starting to uncover the reasons. This anxiety in me tends to happen most often when I recognize a quality in someone that mirrors a quality I see in myself, but it is one that has been a long-standing source of rejection (or possible rejection) for me – and consequently unease. For example, qualities such as being expressive, emotional, imaginative, curious or having a love of learning. Qualities like these are all central to who I am, but I've not always felt at ease with these aspects of myself for various reasons. Chapter 5 looks at personal qualities that are undoubtedly strengths, whilst acknowledging that sometimes these positive attributes can feel complicated.

Let me use being expressive as an example. I value the quality of being expressive in others and in myself, but I've often felt this is something that will lead others to reject me. So, when I see someone else being outwardly (even proudly) expressive and they are not being rejected, and I reciprocate with this quality and I'm not rejected for it, I get an uneasy feeling. It's a kind of 'cognitive dissonance'. It's getting easier with time, which is why I don't avoid people who activate anxiety in me. I have so much to learn, and to enjoy, from being with them.

Trust is the quality in a relationship that reduces this anxiety the most. If I can trust that there is honesty between us – that both of us can share our feelings about the relationship and speak to each other if there is a problem – then I am more likely to relax.

Do interpersonal events, no matter how small they may seem to others, prompt intense emotions for you? Maybe your trackers can help you recognize patterns.

. . . .

. . . .

. . . .

. . . .

. . . .

. . . .

Do some people cause stronger emotional reactions in you than others? Do you have any thoughts about what that could be related to?

. . . .

. . . .

. . . .

. . . .

. . . .

What qualities in a relationship do you think might help you feel less anxious? Is there anything you, or others, could do or say which would be supportive?

. . . .

. . . .

. . . .

. . . .

. . . .

. . . .

Sometimes, I wish I could talk to people about how anxious I feel, but often I feel too worried about their reaction to tell them. Use the next few lines to write down what you wish you could express to people, even if this isn't something you want, or are able, to do at present.

. . . .

. . . .

. . . .

. . . .

. . . .

Routine and schedule

My routine and schedule play a significant role in my emotional regulation and ability to face challenges. I need lots of time alone to feel okay. When my schedule is too full and I don't have enough time by myself, I am vulnerable to panic attacks and insomnia. When I was younger, I prioritized time with my friends above time alone, which made me struggle more with my mental health. I often cancelled plans because I was either on the edge of a panic attack or recovering from one – all red, puffy eyes and embarrassment.

Nowadays, I attempt to plan my time so that it's balanced between all the areas of my life. Now I know that a carefully planned schedule reduces my vulnerability to intense emotions, I prioritize careful planning. I don't always get the balance right, but I try. It's hard to say no sometimes, but it's worth it for me to avoid panic attacks that leave me breathless and crying on the bedroom floor.

It helps me to plan my week and month ahead, including what I'm going to do with any free time. In previous years, my days would take the shape of my mood. If I felt sad, I would stay in bed all day. If I felt ashamed, I would avoid seeing my friends. A plan makes it more likely that my day will be shaped by my values and my goals, not decided by how I feel at any given moment. Chapter 3 explores more on this topic.

How does your schedule and routine affect your emotions?

. . . .

. . . .

. . . .

. . . .

. . . .

. . . .

. . . .

. . . .

Environmental

Whilst some people have significant sensory processing differences – some autistic people for example – we all have sensory preferences that play a part in how we feel. For example, I prefer my home to be tidy so that it's calmer for me visually. I don't like bright overhead lights, especially when I'm tired; and sometimes, I need music off and for it to be quiet. I find it hard to regulate my emotions when I'm cold too. Like many people, I find nature grounding – it reminds me that everything changes and to live in the moment.

What do you find helpful in your environment? Make a list below and feel free to consider aspects such as lighting, sounds, smells, textures, temperatures and aspects of nature.

. . . .

. . . .

. . . .

. . . .

. . . .

. . . .

. . . .

. . . .

. . . .

Physical

We all know that how we're feeling physically affects our emotional state. When I haven't slept well, especially over a longer period of time, I find it harder to regulate my emotions. When I'm physically unwell or in pain, I can slip into a low or anxious mood. Similarly, when I haven't eaten well, I'm liable to get upset or angry quickly. When I was younger, I had an eating disorder for a couple of years. Restricting my food was my way of trying to cope with feelings that I didn't know how to manage – shame, anxiety, feeling different. I no longer have an eating disorder, and I try hard to trust and respond to my hunger signals.

When writing the first draft of this book, some problems arose in my life. Feeling unsure and powerless, I started to restrict my food, exercise more and sleep less. My mood dropped very low and thoughts about self-harm and suicide started happening, as they tend to when I struggle. I felt isolated from people I love and didn't know where to turn because I felt ashamed. After a while, I decided to speak about how distressed I felt, and these conversations compelled me to eat, rest and sleep again. My mood started to improve a few days later.

Some people find that their emotions are influenced by their hor-mones, for example feeling differently at different times in their men-strual cycle (if they have one). Everyone is affected by physical factors differently. Being more sensitive to hunger than others I know used to make me feel like there was something wrong with me, but now I accept it and try to meet my needs as best as I can. Here's space for you to note down how physical factors affect you.

. . . .

. . . .

. . . .

. . . .

. . . .

. . . .

. . . .

. . . .

. . . .

How do your difficulties relate to one another?

When I was newly diagnosed, I didn't understand how my difficulties related to one another. I didn't fully understand how my emotions or sense of identity shifted in relation to how close I felt to someone. Through talking about my difficulties with non-judgemental people and with others who shared similar experiences, I started to picture a web of how my difficulties related to one another (Figure 1.1).

When my mood is low or my shame is strong, I'm more likely to feel anxious about people distancing themselves from me or leaving me. I'm also more likely to respond in ways that make me feel more upset, more down about myself and self-loathing. Conversely, when I feel connected to someone who plays an important part in my life, I feel more relaxed and more compassionate towards myself. By visualizing my difficulties as a web, I was in a better position to start unravelling it.

A happier mood

Feel more confident　　　　　　　　　Reduced anxiety

Feel happier
about who I am ———— Less shame

More trusting of myself and others

**Feel connected
to others**

Confident to socialize and interact　　　　　Feel able to do things more easily,
Can talk easily with others　　　　　　　　　especially with others
Can look others in the eye
Can trust others more easily

More urges to
self-harm
　　　　　　　　　　　　　　　More likely to have suicidal
Shame and embarrassment　　　　　　thoughts

Feel ashamed
about who I am ———— High anxiety

Crying a lot

　　　　　　　　　　　　　　　　　Panic attacks

**Feel disconnected
from others**

Possible paranoid thoughts　　　　　　　　More impulsive actions,
　　　　　　　　　　　　　　　　　　　　e.g. messages on my phone

Painful to socialize and interact　　　　　　　More anxiety
Struggle to trust others or look people in the eye　　More panic
Mask a lot in social situations　　　　　　　　More feeling alone
　　　　　　　　　　　　　　　　　　　　More feeling disconnected

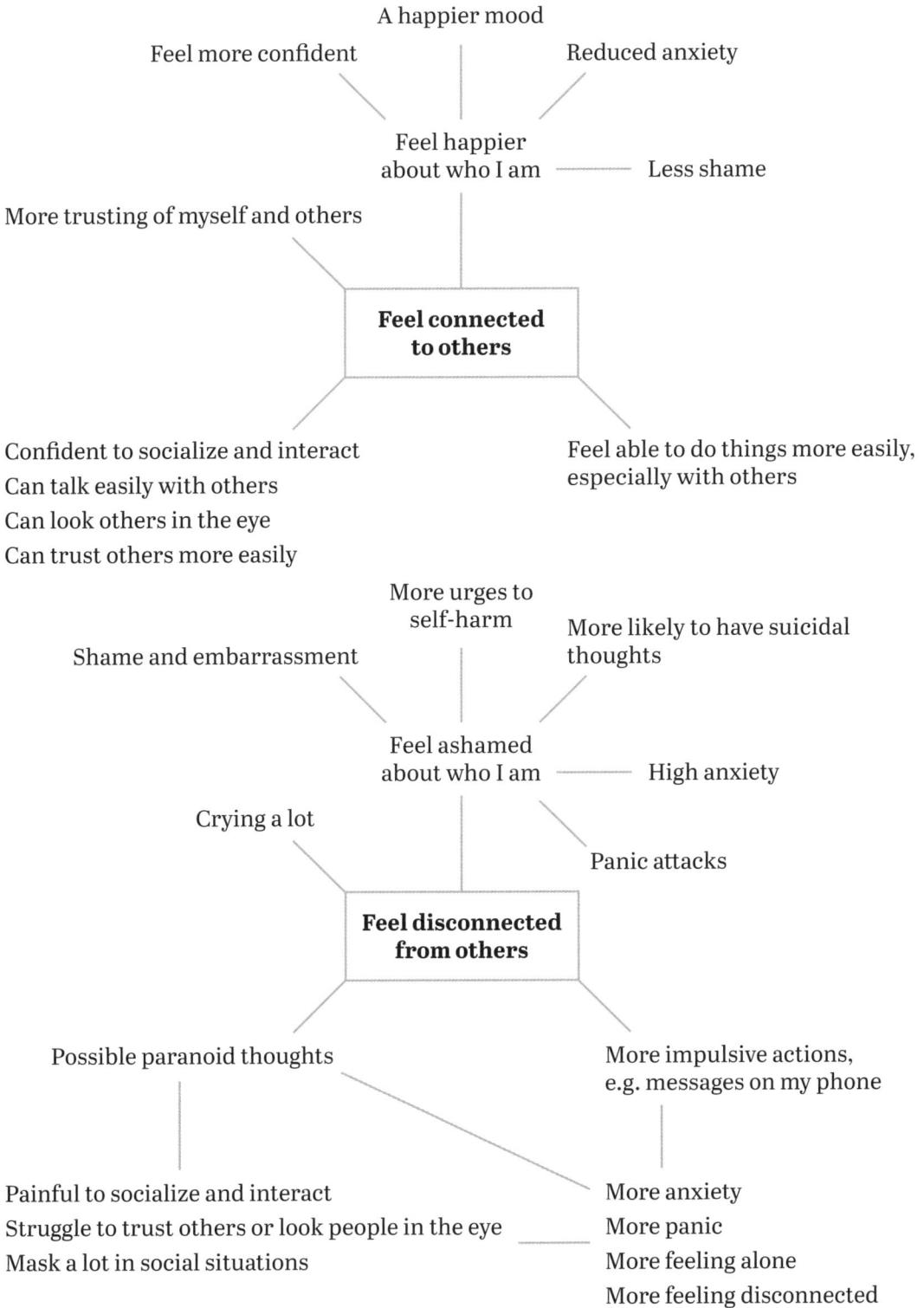

Figure 1.1 My web of difficulties

Here's a space for you to reflect on how your own difficulties might relate to one another. There's no pressure to get it perfect – you can come back and change your ideas at any time.

CHAPTER 2

Caring for Myself
(Even When I Feel Self-Loathing)

My three kinds of self-loathing

'Look after yourself', 'Treat yourself how you would a friend', 'Be kind to yourself' – I'd heard these phrases countless times from people who meant well and cared about me, but I couldn't bring myself to do these things. To do something solely because it improved my mental health was alien to me; to be compassionate towards myself was like trying to speak an unfamiliar language. Three things I could do with my eyes closed though: self-deprivation, self-criticism and self-punishment. Even though it's painful for me to reflect on the three kinds of self-loathing I knew so well, I wanted to share them here and how, over time, I learnt to relate to myself with more compassion and gentleness.

Self-deprivation

I used to deny myself comfort and nourishment, especially rest and food. When I was at secondary school (high school), I would do my school work or revision for hours, setting exhausting goals and promising myself that when I reached these goals I would rest. When I arrived at these goals, I would break the promise I made to myself, telling myself that I hadn't done enough and didn't deserve to rest. It wasn't only studying and revision that I used to deprive myself of basic needs. I did it with exercising, eating and other areas of my life.

People who cared about me told me that I 'needed to stop' and was 'making myself sick', but I didn't know how to stop. I was too scared of what would happen if I stopped being relentless with my goals. What if I didn't do well in my exams? I didn't know how I would cope with my feelings of regret over not studying more. What if I gained weight and people made comments about my body? My identity felt too close to the size and shape of my body that I didn't know how I would handle such remarks. What if I cancelled my plans with my friends because I was too tired? My fear of social disapproval made me ignore my own needs.

As a teenager and young adult, being relentless with my goals gave me a sense of control over my life, future, body and relationships. Depriving myself of rest and food was also one way in which I could physically express how I hated myself so much and how hard it felt for me to live in the world as a person who didn't know how to cope with her emotions. At the time, I blamed myself for not being able to 'stop' as people told me. Now I understand that my inability to 'stop' wasn't a personal failing, but a sign that I needed to learn new ways of relating to myself, to others and living in the world.

Do you deny yourself comfort or nourishment of any kind? Feel free to write your thoughts here.

....

....

....

....

....

....

Self-criticism

When I was a teenager, self-criticism was my main way of talking to myself. My internal monologue was almost constantly harsh: you should be ashamed of yourself, everyone hates you, you're disgusting, you make other people's lives hell, and many other, much crueller, phrases that I don't want to write. The older I got, the wilder my self-criticism grew.

I routinely raged at my face in the mirror, insulting myself for every little flaw I had or mistake I made, whether real or imagined. Berating myself was a ritual for not being able to cope with my emotions. Self-criticism meant I was a constant open wound, but I also believed this kept me safe.

To speak kindly to myself also felt absurd. Why would I allow myself a compassionate internal monologue when I saw myself as a shameful person who made life difficult for others? Self-criticism was also a by-product of growing up feeling different; I didn't know anyone else who struggled like I did with emotions, and I felt alienated by that. Even though I was loved immensely, many of my interests and the rabbit holes I lost myself in didn't match those of others around me. No matter how loved I was, I often felt like I didn't fully belong, and it's lonely to grow up feeling this way.

Is self-criticism a part of your life? How does it look for you?

. . . .

. . . .

. . . .

. . . .

. . . .

. . . .

Self-punishment

Self-harm started for me before the age of ten. I realized, probably by accident, that physical pain had an effect on emotional pain – an effect that I could apply to situations that were difficult for me emotionally. The sensation of physical pain brought me out of my emotional pain temporarily and gave me a feeling of emotional release. By the time I was a young teenager, I realized that releasing my emotions through screaming and yelling usually resulted in more problems for me, so hurting my body physically meant I could release my emotions silently and have fewer immediate problems. I also used self-harm as a punishment for not being able to contain my emotions and 'be like everyone else': *I've hurt others, so I deserve to hurt myself.* I also hoped hurting myself would 'teach me a lesson' which, of course, it didn't.

For me as a young adult, self-harm was a form of masking my emotions. I hurt myself physically to stop myself from having sizable displays of emotion – sobbing or very visible panic attacks – in places I didn't want to, or didn't feel safe to, show my emotions. If something upset me when I was in public or with others, I could go to the bathroom, hurt myself, come out and pretend everything was fine. Throughout my teenage years and throughout my twenties, I've had more visible displays of emotion in public than anyone else I've ever known. I've sat down on street corners crying, had meltdowns in train stations, panic attacks on buses, in shops and cafes. I've felt very exposed.

Nowadays, I don't hurt myself routinely, but it's still sometimes a challenge for me not to hurt myself physically when I get overwhelmed. I know that lots of people with BPD relate to self-harm, so Chapter 3 explores this more. There's a lot of misunderstanding and judgement associated with self-harm; you deserve understanding, to be responded to with an open mind and support. Do you relate to punishing yourself in any way? Feel free to write down any thoughts.

· ·

· ·

· ·

· ·

· ·

· ·

☆ Towards self-compassion
Being kind to yourself can feel difficult

It can feel anxiety-provoking to care for yourself. Here are some common fears associated with moving away from self-hatred towards self-compassion:

☆ that it means you are (or will be seen as being) weak, lazy or self-indulgent

☆ believing that compassion is something others deserve and you don't

☆ thinking it will lead to failure or less success

☆ not knowing how to even begin caring for yourself

☆ feeling painful emotions such as sadness, grief, shame or guilt when you show yourself compassion.

Children learn to be kind to themselves through their own experiences of being cared for and through observing others' kindness (or lack of kindness) towards themselves and others. Being treated throughout childhood and adolescence as though your needs don't matter – or seeing significant others believing their own needs don't matter – can mean we grow into adults who don't feel worthy of being kind to themselves. Often, there is a belief that it's always right to always put others' needs before our own. This is a belief rooted in generosity, but which can leave altruistic individuals depleted themselves.

How easy or difficult do you find it to be kind to yourself and what fears do you have about this? Whilst growing up, what did you learn about being kind to yourself from adults around you?

. . . .

. . . .

. . . .

. . . .

. . . .

. . . .

. . . .

. . . .

. . . .

Looking beyond self-loathing

The first person who taught me to look beyond self-loathing and relate to myself differently was my DBT therapist. It was a far from easy or linear process though. When she told me I needed to treat myself with respect and kindness to reduce the distress I felt, I resisted. First, I argued that I didn't deserve it. Second, I told her that it made me squirm with embarrassment. This is what a typical conversation looked like:

My therapist: "Do you think other people deserve to show themselves kindness?"

Me: "Yes."

Therapist: "Okay, then you deserve the same as others."

Me: "I know what you're saying, but it just feels so wrong for me."

Therapist: "I know, Rosie, but even if it feels uncomfortable for you, you have to go through that discomfort and try it anyway."

Me: "I really don't want to. I feel so embarrassed, and I don't feel like I deserve it."

Therapist: "I know it's something new for you and it feels hard. However, the only way to start believing that you deserve kindness is to start treating yourself as if you do deserve it. If you act first, no matter how uncomfortable this feels, the feeling of deserving it will eventually follow."

It was the 'fake it till you make it' approach – and it felt jarring. I was scared of becoming self-indulgent and worried that people would laugh at me or tell me that I was undeserving. I didn't believe I deserved kindness, but at that point in time I trusted this professional enough to try something new with her support. She helped me take little leaps of faith, small experiments in acting as if I deserved kindness: leaving work a few minutes earlier than usual, not scolding myself for double-texting a friend, asking for something small that I needed, taking a long shower. She taught me that when I had thoughts about being embarrassing, lazy or undeserving, to notice them but see they didn't have to influence my actions. We practised responding to these thoughts aloud like actors reading a script: *Thank you for the thought that I don't deserve this, but I'm going to go ahead and do it anyway!* Like actors rehearsing a play, it took months for me to feel more comfortable with this new way of being and for it to feel less stilted and more natural. My therapist was my audience – a supportive one.

At this time, I entered a temporary season of grief for the times I had deprived myself, hated myself and told myself I was worthless. Sometimes when I was kind to myself – or let others care for me – I would cry as if to acknowledge all those lost opportunities for care. I decided I never wanted to go back to that way of being, even though treating myself kindly is an ongoing process that requires my persistence. On days I feel resistant to being kind to myself, I tell myself that having self-compassion is something I deserve, even if I don't feel it. Treating myself kindly has a regulating effect on my emotions that is worth any initial challenges.

What little leaps or small experiments in acting as if you deserve kindness could you take? Start small and build up. Even if you feel undeserving of kindness, by acting as if you are deserving you will begin to feel more worthy over time. If you're not sure where to start, have a look at the next section first.

. . . .

. . . .

. . . .

. . . .

. . . .

. . . .

Where to start?

If it's your first time thinking about caring for yourself, it might be hard to know even where to begin. Here's an activity you can do using small objects such as pebbles, pegs or small pieces of paper.

1. Take a handful of small objects and place them in a bowl or next to you.

2. Take a few moments to ask yourself: What do I need? What would make me feel cared for? This could be anything, such as time alone, someone to talk to, a walk in nature, practical help around the house, etc.

3. Write these ideas on your small objects, even if they are tentative thoughts or feel uncomfortable.

4. Display your small items somewhere you will see them throughout your week. Use them to prompt your thinking about what you might need and what small acts of caring for yourself you could explore. Add to your collection if anything else comes to mind throughout your week.

5. Whenever you feel slightly – even tentatively – ready to experiment with one of these acts of kindness towards yourself, seize the moment. For example, if your chosen small object is about connection, then act on it by messaging a friend asking them to go for a coffee. Don't wait until you feel fully ready as this moment may never come!

6. Even if you don't feel like you deserve it, act as if you do deserve it and the believing part will catch up over time.

Here is space to note down your small experiments in acting as if you deserve kindness, including what you needed, what you did, how you felt during and how you felt after. Taking these small steps, caring for yourself will over time start to feel less performative and more instinctive.

Date	What I needed	What I did	How I felt during	How I felt afterwards

Care for the body, care for the mind

The relationship between body and the mind is complex and one that others can articulate more eloquently than me. One thing's for sure though, looking after the body as best as we can tends to have a positive effect on our emotional state. Of course, illness happens and bodies do unpredictable things; however, if we've eaten well, slept enough, had a shower, had a balance of rest and exercise then we tend to feel better mentally than when those things have not happened.

Are there any things you could do to look after yourself physically? Use the chart on the next page to help you reflect on this.

Take a look at your emotion trackers. Do you feel differently if you have looked after yourself physically compared to times you haven't? It can be really hard to look after yourself physically, especially if you are feeling low. What might help you care for your body more consistently?

What could I do to care for myself physically?	When and how often?	What impact might this have on me emotionally?

☆ Dialectics: Towards balance

People spoke to me a lot about 'balance' when I was younger: 'You should find a balance between work and rest' or simply 'You need more balance in your life'. Like the idea of caring for myself, the idea of 'finding a balance' felt impossible. It would mean letting go of my 'all-or-nothing' approach to life – and that felt too scary. DBT changed that for me though.

As the name suggests, dialectical behaviour therapy has the idea of 'dialectics' at its core. If you've studied philosophy, you may have heard of dialectics in relation to the Ancient Greek philosophers Socrates and Plato. These philosophers valued sharing opposing ideas as a back-and-forth dialogue with one another and discussed their ideas until they reached a conclusion that considered both points of view. The concept of dialectics in DBT is similar. It refers to the idea that two opposite, or seemingly conflicting, ideas can both be true at the same time.

Here are a few examples of opposite, seemingly conflicting, ideas that can both be true at the same time:

- ☆ I need to rest, and I need to work.
- ☆ I can care for myself and care for others.
- ☆ I am strong, and I am vulnerable.
- ☆ I can smile, and I can cry.
- ☆ I can help others and still struggle myself.
- ☆ I can be open and also have boundaries.
- ☆ I can be independent, and I can ask for help.

And perhaps most famously in DBT:

- ☆ I can accept myself as I am, and I can work towards change.

A key concept in DBT is that by balancing these opposites we can live more effectively. In the context of DBT, living effectively tends to mean being able to cope with life's challenges without doing things that hurt our body, health, relationships, and so on, and being able to work towards our own definition of a fulfilling life. Like Plato and Socrates who discussed opposing ideas until they reached a conclusion that considered both points of view, in DBT opposite statements can be synthesized – fused together – to create a more balanced, more nuanced statement. For example, *I must always work, and I must always rest* can be synthesized into a more balanced notion: *I need a mix of work and rest in my life.*

Dialectics was an eye-opener for me. Whilst living in the extremes made me feel safe, it also depleted me. But as I no longer wanted to live in emotional agony, I had to let go of my 'all-or-nothing' approach to life and embrace the nuances of 'both', 'a little bit' 'and the 'middle ground' – no matter how scary that felt. Questions were one way of creating space for me to think more dialectically, for example:

☆ What would another perspective on this be?
☆ Am I seeing the whole story or just part of it?
☆ Would this idea be true always or just sometimes?
☆ What nuances might I be missing?
☆ What might the consequences be of not thinking dialectically?

Do you tend to think, and live, in an 'all-or-nothing' manner? What does that look like for you and how does it feel to live this way?

. . . .

. . . .

. . . .

. . . .

. . . .

. . . .

. . . .

. . . .

How do you feel about the idea of thinking, and living, more dialectically? How might it feel to have more balance in your approach to life?

. . . .

. . . .

. . . .

. . . .

. . . .

. . . .

Here's space to write down some of your own pairs of opposing ideas and combine them into a more balanced, dialectical statement which synthesizes the two.

Opposing statements

1. . . . .

. . . .

2. . . . .

. . . .

What might a more dialectical statement be which synthesizes these two opposing statements?

. . . .

. . . .

. . . .

. . . .

Opposing statements

1. . . . .

. . . .

2. . . . .

. . . .

What might a more dialectical statement be which synthesizes these two opposing statements?

. . . .

. . . .

. . . .

. . . .

Opposing statements

1. . . . .

. . . .

2. . . . .

. . . .

What might a more dialectical statement be which synthesizes these two opposing statements?

. . . .

. . . .

. . . .

. . . .

Opposing statements

1. . . . .

. . . .

2. . . . .

. . . .

What might a more dialectical statement be which synthesizes these two opposing statements?

. . . .

. . . .

. . . .

. . . .

☆ Self-expression

One of the most effective ways I can care for myself is through expressing myself. Whilst I can't find any research on the theme of self-expression for people with this diagnosis, after countless conversations with individuals, it seems self-expression is commonly a strong need. I put this down to two reasons. First, people with this diagnosis often relate to growing up in 'invalidating environments' (Linehan 1993). These may have been environments which shamed them – whether directly or indirectly, intentionally or unintentionally – for sharing their thoughts and feelings. Second, people with this diagnosis often feel unable to speak openly about their lives due to fear of judgement, loss of reputation, relationships, livelihood, and so on.

I have always kept diaries and journals as a space to express my thoughts and feelings. I wrote and drew like my life depended on it – and often it felt like it did. My notebooks never judged me; no matter what I wanted to tell them or how long I needed them to listen to me. Now I understand myself and life is wildly different. My diaries and journals are not for my survival; I need them to help me live life to the fullest, but (thankfully) I don't need them to stay alive.

How do you feel about self-expression? Is it important to you?

....

....

....

....

....

....

....

....

Ideas for self-expression

If self-expression is important to you or you are keen to explore how it might help you, here are some ideas. I hope you'll find solace in these ideas if you've ever been told that it was wrong, shameful, silly or self-indulgent to express yourself. Expressing yourself is none of these things. It's a natural, understandable and entirely human want and need. It also can be confidence-giving, empowering, life-affirming, fun and a way to deepen the connections with yourself and with others.

If you've ever felt unsafe to express yourself, then getting started can be unsettling. For some people, the unease may feel manageable and ultimately fruitful. For others, it can be really challenging at first. In the past, I wrote, drew and spoke about parts of myself and my life that made me feel overwhelmed, feeling unsafe in my own mind and body. It's important to feel safe and in control when you express yourself. There is no need to push yourself.

It's also worth acknowledging that self-expression is for you and you only, unless you choose to share it with someone else you trust. In Chapter 5, we will explore people who make you feel safe.

Voice recorder app

During a difficult period in my life, when I was struggling with insomnia, feeling isolated and suicidal thoughts, I used the voice recorder app on my phone to talk about what was on my mind. It brought relief to get my thoughts out of my head. I played it back to myself and tried to reflect as an objective listener: What was I going through? What was happening? What could I say to myself?

With voice recorder apps, you don't have to listen back if you don't want to, and you can click delete at any point. You could use a voice recorder app to share what's on your mind. Alternatively, if you feel able, you could make a message of encouragement to play back when you need it.

Letter

Letter-writing is becoming an increasingly rare artform. However, it's one with endless potential for self-expression. After all, people have been writing letters for thousands of years to express, and share, their thoughts, ideas and emotions. Letters are often tucked inside envelopes away from curious eyes – and you don't ever have to send them if you don't want to or if that wouldn't be useful. Here are some ideas for letter writing for you to explore if you fancy:

- ☆ letter to a friend or supportive person (can be imagined) asking for advice and support
- ☆ letter sharing all the things you want to let go
- ☆ letter of gratitude saying thank you to someone or something
- ☆ letter to yourself as a child
- ☆ letter to yourself in the future
- ☆ letter containing your hopes and dreams
- ☆ letter expressing all the thoughts circling through your mind.

Zine making

Zines (pronounced like the zine in 'magazine') are self-published, low-cost, informal texts involving words and/or images. They are often created by folding a piece of paper several times and stapling it to make a booklet. Zines tend to be one-off texts or reproduced in small batches by a photocopier or a home printer and often use materials found around the home, like ephemera, old tickets or stickers. Makers of zines often enjoy an unruly, joyful creative process, embracing mistakes, smudges or tears as part of the beauty and authenticity of the finished product. They are a brilliant low-stakes, low-pressure project for self-expression. Not only that though, zines also have a rich legacy as 'resistant media' (Piepmeier 2009).

Perhaps you would like to make your own zine, maybe as your own form of resistance. Zine makers have often challenged established ideas and norms through their works, so you will be in good company. Alternatively, as zines are also associated with fan culture, perhaps you might like to make a zine expressing some of the things you enjoy most?

Poetry

I love poetry, whether writing, reading, listening to it or even performing it. It gives me a thrill that something as small as a poem, made only of words, can evoke moods, express complex ideas, contain memories or be a call to action.

A common misconception about poetry is that it has to 'be' a certain way. There is no right or wrong way to make a poem. If you have an idea, feeling, thought or memory that you want to capture, then you could try creating a poem. Here are a few of my ideas if you want some inspiration for getting started:

☆ Using the five senses as a structure, describe a sight, sound, smell, taste and sensation. This could relate to where you are right now or to an imagined place.

☆ A conversation you want to have but haven't yet been able to have. Maybe you could start with the words 'I want to tell you' or 'If we could talk, this is what I would say'.

☆ A lesson you learned that you want others to know. Perhaps it's something you learned the hard way.

☆ If emotions could speak, what would they say? Anger would say…
Sadness would say… Joy would say… Love would say…, and so on.
What colour, smell, sound and texture would they have?

☆ Ten things that make you laugh/smile/cry/angry/blush. Ten things
you are grateful for/wish for/long for.

Collage

For this one you need some paper, such as old magazines, wrapping
paper or ephemera, and some glue and scissors, unless you prefer to
tear the paper. Explore which colours, images, shapes or words appeal
to you, then cut or rip them as you like. Assemble your pieces and stick
them down as you wish. You can glue them all down straight away, one
by one or try out different arrangements before committing to glue.

As art psychotherapist Anila Babla explains in 'Putting the pieces
together: Collage as a mode in the treatment of trauma' there are 'potential therapeutic benefits of collage' (2020). She describes that trauma is
'commonly associated with the fragmentation of memory' and 'collage
is concerned with integration, the counterfoil to fragmentation if you
will'. She also notes that collage is 'an artform with roots in protest' (as
with zines and poetry).

☆ Comfort

Having BPD can feel unbearable at times. The first layer is the overwhelming emotions, the second is the worry about whether you will be
taken seriously and treated with respect. The third layer is that it can be
lonely too. In the UK, the diagnoses of PTSD, OCD, depression, bipolar
disorder and eating disorders all have charities with supportive online
resources and dedicated helplines, but not BPD. Furthermore, BPD is
rarely shown in an accurate light in the media or the arts. There are lots
of public figures and celebrities sharing personal experiences of mental
health conditions, including depression, anxiety, eating disorders, and
more, but very few sharing personal experience of BPD.

I wanted to take a moment to share three tools that I hope will bring comfort to you when you need it most. I know these are a form of caring for yourself, so they may feel tricky at first. However, I hope that you – along with the many others reading this book and facing similar struggles – can take some little leaps and try out some of these things.

Inner child

Various concepts of the 'inner child' are woven throughout different types of therapy, books on psychology, as well as myths and stories around the world. What I mean by inner child, though, is the notion that we were all once a child and we can call upon that idea or those memories. One of the first images that comes to my mind when I think of myself as a child is a photograph of me smelling a rose. Perhaps because my name is Rosie, the image of 'little me' smelling this flower has been strong. How about you? Do any images, thoughts or impressions come to mind of 'little you'? I understand this might not be easy, and you can take all the time you need.

. . . .

. . . .

. . . .

. . . .

If you were going to speak to 'little you', what would your voice sound like? How would you position your body? If 'little you' needed help with something or was worried about something, how would you speak to them? What would you say and how would you say it?

. . . .

. . . .

. . . .

. . . .

You may find it easier to be compassionate towards the idea of a 'little you', than it is to speak gently to yourself as an adult. Try to take moments throughout the day to think about 'little you' and see if it helps you speak with more gentleness towards yourself. If you find it upsetting to think of yourself as a child, perhaps because it brings up difficult feelings, then you could either think of an imaginary child, character or an animal that elicits caring feelings.

Take a moment to draw or write about 'little you' (or this other child, character or animal).

Self-validation

We have explored 'invalidating environments' and how people with BPD are often no stranger to phrases like 'Stop crying!' 'Don't be so sensitive' or 'Why are you so dramatic?', Words spoken by others, especially when we were young, tend to become the words we say inwardly to ourselves. For me, I find comfort in telling myself things like:

- ☆ 'It's okay to feel things deeply.'
- ☆ 'It's okay to be a sensitive and emotional person.'
- ☆ 'I'm allowed to be upset/angry/sad about this.'
- ☆ 'My emotions are genuine and legitimate.'

What words might bring you comfort? Try telling yourself these regularly. The more you say them to yourself, the more natural they will feel and the easier it will be to use them when emotions are intense.

. . . .

. . . .

. . . .

. . . .

. . . .

Safe place

When my stress levels get too high, thoughts about suicide and self-harm arise. These thoughts are one of my signals that I'm approaching a crisis. When I notice these thoughts, I need to step away from my problems, even briefly, until I can take more steps to feel better. Whilst we explore coping with feeling very distressed in Chapter 3, I wanted to share the idea of a 'safe place' now because a safe place can be evoked in your mind at any time and in any place to bring comfort.

Is there a place that makes you feel safe, happy or calm? It can be a real place or imagined. In the mindmap below write down any words that come to mind which are associated with this place.

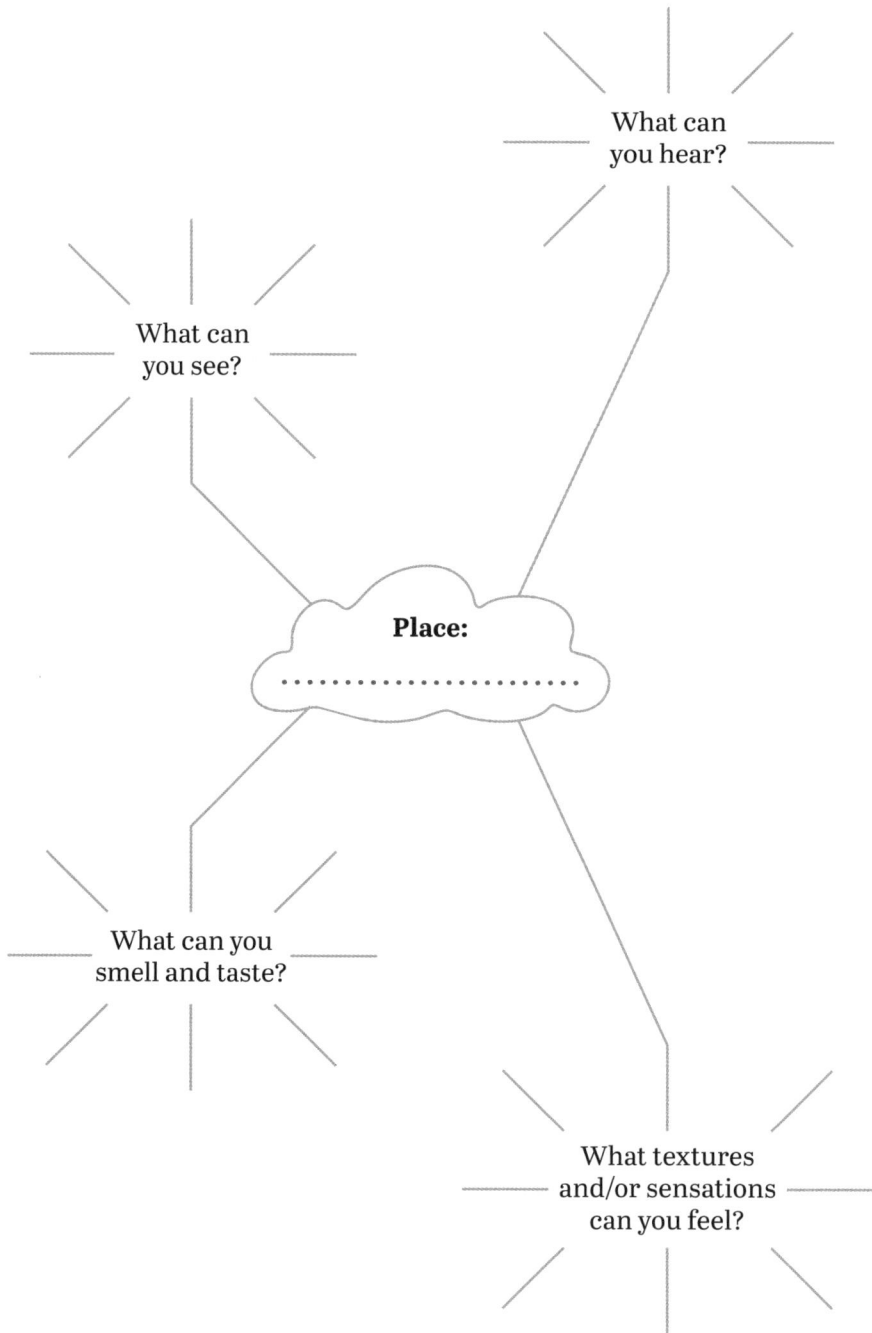

What can
you hear?

What can
you see?

Place:

· ·

What can you
smell and taste?

What textures
and/or sensations
can you feel?

If you prefer to draw as well as (or instead of) writing then here is space for you to do this.

Why not take a few moments during your day to imagine being in this place? If there's something tangible to help bring this place to life in your mind, such as an object connected to this place, music, photos, video, or even scents, then feel free to use these to help make your safe place feel more real.

An alternative to an imagined safe place is listening to sleep stories on apps or YouTube. Sleep stories tend to be set in relaxing places and involve gentle themes, minimal plots and nothing to worry their listeners. Although they are designed to help with insomnia, listening to them during the day can offer a much-needed break.

CHAPTER 3

Coping with Intense Emotions

(and Surviving Moments that Feel Impossible)

Feeling emotions strongly, even at an intensity that feels physically painful, is at the core of BPD. Sometimes, having my emotions playing on full volume makes me feel excited, energized and in love with life. In the past, when my emotions were far less regulated than today, my friends would notice this in my laughter, how energetically I danced, how excitedly I spoke and my enthusiasm for life. It didn't always feel pleasant though; it often felt strangely painful, and then a low would arrive; crying would turn to sobbing, tiredness to exhaustion and embarrassment to a hot rash of shame that made me want to hide from everyone I loved.

Even when I wasn't cycling through these highs and lows, an emotion could jolt me, out of nowhere, like an electric shock. Someone could say something to me, or I would remember something, and there it was – a surge of emotion coursing through my body. Embarrassment and shame were, and still are, the most easily activated emotions in me. Being social emotions, embarrassment and shame tend to occur in social contexts: *Did I upset them? Did I overstep their boundaries? Do they want me to leave? Did I say too much?* I often tried to mask how I felt, but pushing down emotions would intensify their force until they became impossible to contain without my distress showing. Often, they came out in huge panic attacks of crying and hyperventilating in my bedroom.

☆ Learning to cope with intense emotions

Before we take a closer look at intense emotions, I want to mention self-harm and suicide. I know emotions may feel so overwhelming at times that self-harm and suicide can come into the picture. Suicide and self-harm, two distinct things not to be confused with one another, can arise for so many reasons. Self-harm may relate to translating emotional pain into physical pain to make it feel more bearable, it may provide a temporary distraction to emotional pain or create sensations when someone feels numb or empty, or it may act as a self-punishment. Suicide may be associated with wanting to escape life that feels too painful or hopelessness that feels insurmountable. If you're struggling, I want you to do everything you can to ask for support – even if you've tried asking before and didn't get the response you needed. I've been there and know it hurts. I really hope you can reach out, whether for the first time or not. There are helplines listed in the 'Support and Resources' section of this book, which I hope can be helpful to you.

As I shared before, I've experienced self-harm and feeling suicidal countless times. Sometimes, my emotional pain felt easier to manage as physical pain, and my suicidal thoughts were generally related to feeling alone, disconnected from people in my life and shameful. Whilst I cannot know exactly how you feel as everyone is different, I keep in mind that people who experience self-harm and suicidal thoughts often feel alone, disconnected and ashamed. Personal themes of feeling unlovable, worthless or helpless, being misunderstood or incorrectly perceived, having no outlet for aspects of identity or emotions are common.

Throughout this chapter I keep all of this in mind, sharing the ways I have strengthened my self-compassion and forged connections with others and the world around me. Some of the ways of coping with intense emotions that I share in this chapter are based on acceptance, whereas others are about trying to gently change emotions. A central dialectic in DBT is acceptance and change: I accept myself, and I change myself. I accept my emotions, and I change them.

I encourage you to familiarize yourself with this chapter when you're not experiencing overwhelming emotions to give yourself a chance to explore and learn. It takes time to learn new ways of relating to yourself and to your emotions; not knowing how to do something and making mistakes is part of the learning process. Play around with the acceptance-based approaches and change-based approaches at different times and for different contexts to see what is most effective in certain scenarios. Feel free to be creative and adapt them to you and your life: this chapter is inspiration not an instruction manual.

Before we begin, take a moment to write yourself a message of encouragement to help you with the learning involved in this chapter. I know encouraging yourself can feel strange at first, but I hope you will gently give it a try.

. . . .

. . . .

. . . .

. . . .

☆ Accepting intense emotions
'Sitting with' emotions

One of the most effective ways of handling intense emotions is to not run from them and not try to make them disappear. Mental health professionals often like to call this 'sitting with emotions' which to me is an accurate description. It's a bit like inviting them, metaphorically, to join you for a cup of tea and a biscuit. The mindset shift I had to make here was to see my emotions as my friends, not my enemies. Friends who had something important to tell me.

As I wrote in Chapter 1, emotions have functions, including communicating key messages. But when emotions hit at full force and it feels distressing, how can we make enough space to listen to what they might be telling us? I'm going to share some of what I've learnt from DBT and also acceptance and commitment therapy (ACT) that enables me to 'sit with' emotions and relate to them as friends, rather than enemies I need to repel.

☆ *Acknowledge that emotions cannot hurt you.* Make a statement to yourself like: *'I am safe.'* Sometimes it feels like anger will make us spontaneously combust, sadness will break our heart, or anxiety will make us 'lose our minds', but emotions don't have that power. What statements might be useful for you to hear when you're feeling like emotions will overwhelm you? Write them below.

. . . .

. . . .

. . . .

. . . .

. . . .

. . . .

. . . .

☆ *Ground yourself.* Intense emotions and their associated bodily responses, such as sweating or a racing heart, can compel us to act without thinking. I know when I'm experiencing intense emotions, my thoughts race and I want to move fast. Have a think about what body positions make you feel calmest and most grounded. For me, it could be sitting, lying or standing depending on how I'm feeling. Allow yourself to move gently if you need to. Put words to your physical experience, such as: *'My feet are on the floor.' 'My back is against the chair.'* or *'My hands are in my lap.'* The act of allowing yourself to adopt a comfortable body position and notice it can put space between you and your emotions. Practise this now and note down your experience.

· ·

· ·

· ·

· ·

· ·

· ·

· ·

☆ *Anchor to the world with your senses.* Do your thoughts take on a more stressful quality when your emotions are intense? *Oh no, what if this all goes wrong? How can I be so ridiculous? Why is everything so awful?* Using your senses to tune in to the world can create space between yourself and what's going on for you emotionally. Ask yourself questions like: *What can I feel beneath my feet? What are my hands touching? Can I smell anything? What colours can I see?* Try to label your experience with objective statements rather than judgements. For example, a train might be 'busy' but not 'awful'. Practise this by writing down what your senses are experiencing at this moment, using objective statements rather than judgements.

· ·

· ·

· ·

· ·

· ·

· ·

· ·

☆ *Just as you observed your body position and surroundings, notice your emotions and thoughts.* The key is to label them without judging them as good, bad, silly, wrong, etc. The phrases 'I notice' and 'I observe' are helpful for noting facts without assigning a value to them: *I notice that I am feeling angry. I observe my thoughts racing. I notice thoughts about rejection and worthlessness.* I liken this to catching a fish in a net and noticing its qualities without judging it as good, bad, ugly or beautiful, etc.

Cognitive defusion: Creating space

Noticing what's going on for you emotionally without judging yourself can create space between you as a person and what you're feeling and thinking. Creating this space can reduce the power that our emotions and thoughts have over us and make them feel less overwhelming. Psychologists refer to this act as cognitive 'defusion', and it is a key technique in acceptance and commitment therapy (ACT). It is called 'defusion' because it involves 'de-fusing' – as in no longer being fused with – thoughts.

There are many cues psychologists use to help individuals practise cognitive defusion. These cues tend to involve images that involve movement, because emotional landscapes are rarely still – even if thoughts and emotions recur, they are always moving. Common examples of cues for cognitive defusion include imagining thoughts as leaves floating down a stream, trains passing through a station or clouds scudding across the sky.

Alternatively, some professionals advise adding the words 'I am noticing that...' or 'My mind is telling me that...' before describing the emotion or the content of the thought. The box below is for you to draw your emotions and thoughts as separate from yourself as a person, perhaps using any of the cues mentioned above if they resonate with you.

ACTIVITY: IMAGINE YOUR THOUGHTS AND EMOTIONS AS A CHARACTER

One way I create space between myself and my thoughts and emotions is to imagine them as a character. I stumbled across this way of gaining distance between myself and my emotional experiences whilst drawing in my journals. At that time, I was struggling with a claustrophobic sense of shame and self-consciousness. I found myself drawing crows in my sketchbooks, with disheveled feathers and broken beaks. These birds were metaphors for my most painful feelings, helping me begin to understand my emotional landscape.

Over time, I drew more characters that took on lighter, gentler colours and personalities representing qualities like hope and self-compassion. Light was seeping around the scratchy inky crow.

Here is a space for you to draw any creatures (real or imaginary) that represent different aspects of your emotional experience. Remember, these are just for you unless you choose to share them with anyone.

'You shouldn't be feeling this way'

Has anyone ever told you that you 'shouldn't be feeling this way' or that you have 'no reason' to feel the things you feel? Have you also ever said these things to yourself? It's common, and understandable, to internalize such invalidating statements, especially if they were expressed by people in positions of power, such as parents, teachers or healthcare professionals. During a crisis, a health professional once told me that I had 'nothing to feel suicidal about'. Their statement echoed years of telling myself that I 'shouldn't' have mental health problems and that I was ungrateful and selfish because I struggled. My pain was amplified by believing I had 'no reason' to feel distressed. It then morphed from being bearable to unbearable – *How dare you be so spoilt. You don't deserve this life. Shame on you*, and so on – until suicidal thoughts and self-harm entered the scene.

Over the years, I've realized that there is no place for 'shoulds' and 'should-nots' when it comes to emotions: we feel how we feel. Emotional lives involve complex mechanics with many moving parts. 'Shoulds' and 'should-nots' layer guilt and shame on to an already heavy weight of emotion. If mental health was as simple as having a ticklist – friends, family, education, work – then I wouldn't be writing this book. Similarly, there is no 'type' of person who experiences mental health problems and no specific 'look'. I've lost count of how many times people have been shocked when I disclose my difficulties. A maxim I live by is that you can never tell what someone is going through unless they tell you.

Are there any 'should' and 'should-not' statements you would like to let go? Note them in the cloud below and see if you can imagine them floating away. Don't worry if you can't imagine this vividly, it's more about the intention to release these from your way of thinking. If they come back, that's entirely normal, and you can imagine them drifting away again. Do this letting go as many times as you need to, without judging yourself.

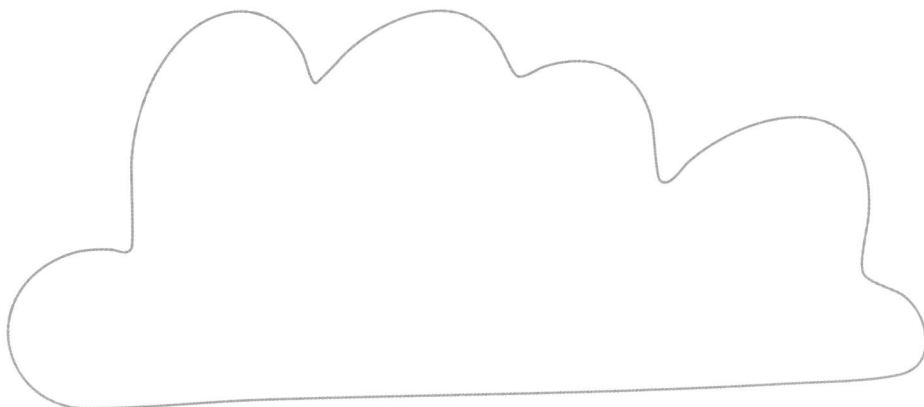

Validation: A breath of fresh air!

A refreshing antidote to 'shoulds' and 'should-nots' when it comes to emotions is validation. Dr Linehan noted that, when a therapist is validating someone, they do the following things. First of all, they 'actively accept' what the person is telling them, and then they communicate that their 'responses make sense'. Next, the therapist takes their 'responses seriously' and does 'not discount or trivialize' (Linehan 1993). It's not just therapists that can validate how someone is feeling – anyone can do it, and it can even be done by yourself for yourself.

Validation involves first recognizing and acknowledging an emotional experience: 'I can see you're upset by what has happened.' Then communicating that an emotional experience is allowed: 'You are allowed to feel upset. It's okay to cry.' Finally, validation is about understanding that an emotional experience is happening for a reason, even if the reason doesn't seem logical or obvious: 'It's understandable to be upset.' 'It makes sense that you feel this way given what you have been through in the past.' The reason may be private, not yet known or involving events or experiences that happened in a person's past.

Validation is often thought of as agreeing with someone, but validating someone does not necessarily mean agreeing with them. It's possible to acknowledge someone's emotions, communicate that they are allowed to feel them and that it's an understandable response (even if you don't know the history) without agreeing with someone's opinions or interpretation of what is happening. My husband validates me all the time, even though he doesn't necessarily think what I am saying is true. Let me share an example. If I'm crying because I think a friend is about to walk out of my life, my husband will let me feel my feelings, communicate that I'm allowed to cry and that he can see why I'm upset, all whilst (kindly) disagreeing with my assessment of the situation.

Validation is a breath of fresh air for people with intense emotions, especially individuals who have spent time in, or still are in, invalidating environments. It allows emotions to pass in their own time, rather than intensifying them, and also increases feelings of connection between people. It's a beautiful, and surprisingly rare, gift to allow a person to feel the way they feel in someone else's presence. Validation is also something you can do for yourself, although it may feel strange at first. On the leaf below write some validating statements that you can try sharing with yourself. Some examples are: *I am allowed to feel upset. It's okay to feel angry. I let myself feel all my feelings.*

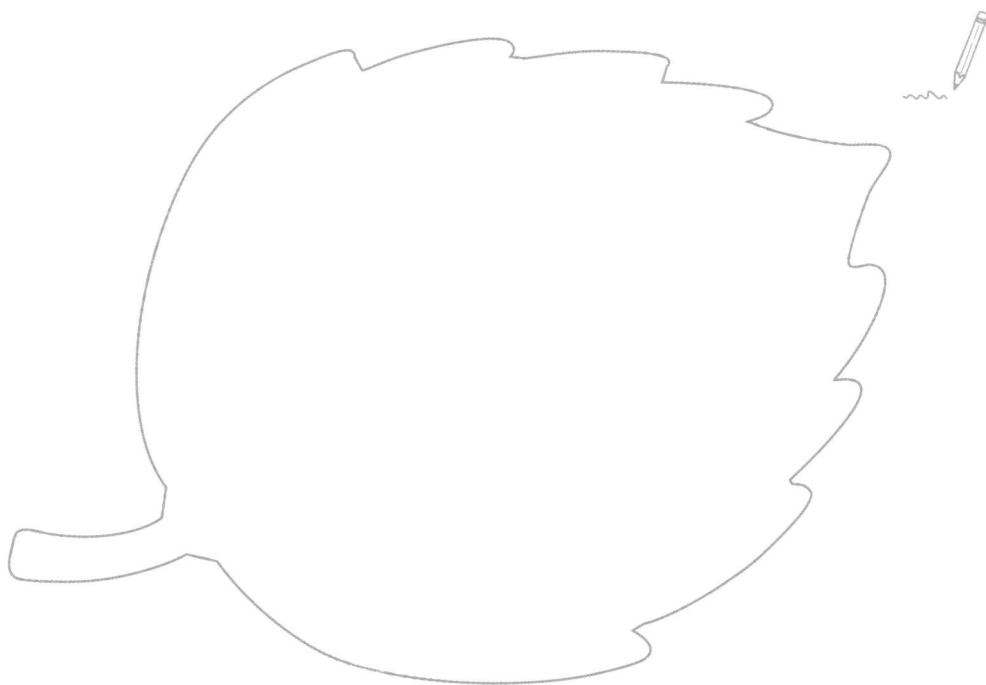

Emotions are like waves

Like waves, emotions build over time: after a while they rise to a peak and then they fall again. Sometimes, an emotion is like a gentle wave and its amplitude feels manageable. Other times, an emotion is like a huge wave and its amplitude feels overwhelming. When I feel an intense emotion, it sometimes feels like its momentum and power will never stop growing and I will be pulled under by it. If you relate to this experience, take a moment to draw a picture of yourself and one of your waves of emotion. When I think of myself in relation to my towering waves of emotion, I feel very small compared.

RIDING THE WAVE

The idea of riding waves of emotion runs through DBT. Riding a wave of emotion is about acknowledging that an emotion will rise, reach its peak and then fall. To ride the wave, the first step is to notice what's happening. Put words to your emotion and describe any associated physical sensations or urges: *I feel a wave of shame coming over me. I feel hot and I'm blushing. I want to run and hide.*

Allow this emotional experience to take place within you. Don't try to push the wave away or shrink it, as this will likely make it intensify. Equally, don't do anything that will actively grow the wave. For example, if you're feeling shame, don't mentally revisit your list of most embarrassing moments. The word 'allow' is important here: you are letting the wave run its natural course without intervening. Acknowledge that you are safe by telling yourself *I am safe.* Remind yourself that the emotion will rise, reach its peak and then fall. Another wave may come, but keep riding these waves until they settle.

Here are some wave outlines that rise, reach their peak and then fall. Feel free to write on these outlines, noting how you felt and what happened.

SURFING URGES

Another related DBT skill is known as 'urge surfing'. Just as riding a wave of emotion is about allowing an emotion to pass without intensifying it, urge surfing is about noticing an urge, not acting on it, and allowing it to lessen in its own time. Strong urges often accompany intense emotions – and this is only natural as emotions have evolved over millennia to ensure the survival of the human species. Sometimes, acting on these urges is essential; and other times, it's detrimental.

The urges I find hardest to resist relate to messaging on my phone. When I'm anxious about my relationships, I get urges to send messages to try to find out whether someone is annoyed or upset with me. Acting on these urges is not helpful for me, because it can negatively affect my relationships; friends can become confused by my question or worried they did something to cause me to feel anxious. These messages feed my anxiety, because, if I do get a reply, I tend to feel guilty for my message, which in turn heightens my anxiety. The response is also usually not 'enough' to reassure me and creates a new urge to apologize or 'check' something else.

Do you struggle with strong urges when you experience intense emotions? What themes do you notice? Do you tend to act on them or not?

. . . .

. . . .

. . . .

. . . .

Surfing an urge is similar to riding a wave of emotion. First of all, notice the urge and put words to it, perhaps starting with *I am having the urge to* . . . . Second, allow the urge to be present. Don't try to push it away or judge yourself for having the urge – it's natural for urges to accompany intense emotions. Just as waves of emotion need time to fall, so do urges. Give yourself time. With each urge surfed, the easier it will feel. The intensity of each urge is likely to decrease over time too.

Here are some wave outlines that rise, reach their peak and then fall. Feel free to write on these waves, noting what your urge was, what you felt compelled to do and what happened as a result of surfing the urge rather than acting on it.

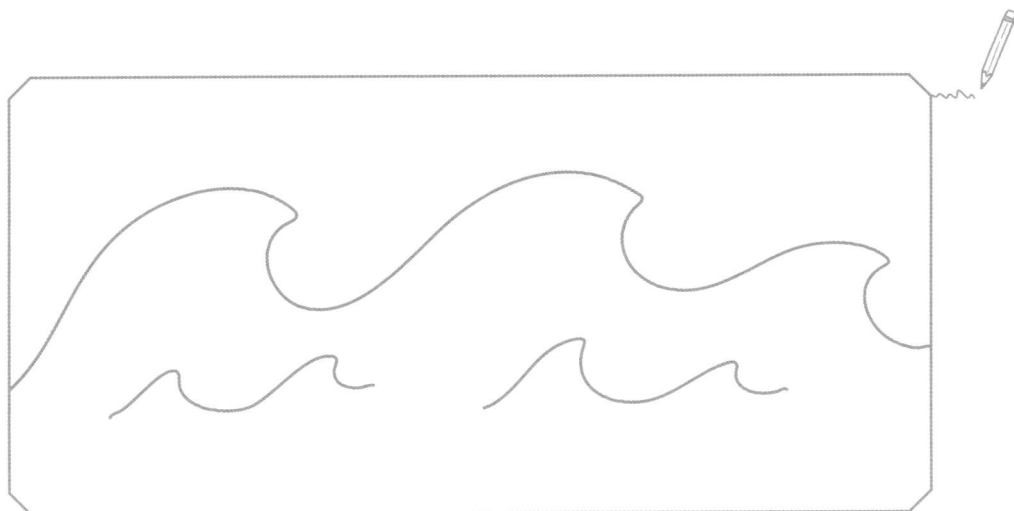

The spaces in between

Have you ever noticed the spaces in between one breath and the next? Or the spaces between the end of a word, or a sentence, and the one that follows? At the end of each wave of emotion there is a pause too, whether long or short, before the next one begins. Within these pauses – between breaths, words, emotions and so on – nothing is happening, and there is a moment of peace.

Over the years, noticing what I call these 'spaces in between' has helped me through all manner of situations. I even used this idea of the spaces in between when I was in labour with my daughter. Each contraction was like a wave that peaked and then fell, followed by an instance of nothingness where I could rest, momentarily, before the next contraction rose. The knowledge that each wave would be followed by a pause made the pain of each one bearable. I use this idea to help calm my social anxiety too. Noticing the natural gaps between utterances in conversations helps me stay calm. Similarly, when I'm having a hectic day, I try to find a space in between the events of the day to take a brief pause.

What 'spaces in between' can you notice in your life? What could you do to acknowledge them more?

. . . .

. . . .

. . . .

. . . .

Keep on going regardless

Sometimes, people ask me how I keep going with so many areas of my life – my work as a teacher, my family, my relationship with my husband, my friends, my writing, and so on. The question I tend to ask myself is though: How come emotions and thoughts like *you're worthless, you don't belong here, you're shameful* don't stop me from living my life in the way I want?

The simple answer is that I acknowledge how I feel and then remind myself that my emotional experience on the inside doesn't have to determine my actions on the outside; regardless of the emotions and thoughts that often confront me, I decide to keep on going. Sometimes, I even think it's because of the emotions and thoughts that I keep going – I don't want shame, anxiety and sadness to call the shots on how I live my life. I let the emotions sit inside me – and I carry on with what I'm doing regardless. It's like walking through freezing rain and reaching the mountaintop even though halfway up your shoes broke.

Recently, I arranged to have lunch with a new friend, and the night beforehand my anxiety became loud and unruly. My thoughts were peppered with 'they don't actually like you', 'shame on you for suggesting this' and 'you're wasting their time'. I had multiple urges to cancel. I decided to let myself feel this embarrassment and fear – I let it sit within me – and meet my friend anyway. I had committed to meeting them, and I also acknowledged to myself that one of my values is about nurturing my friendships: I value connections, and I want to live by my values. I felt anxious, I probably even looked anxious, but I did it nonetheless – I also had a great time. I highly recommend the work of Russ Harris (the founder of acceptance and commitment therapy) on living in accordance with your values if you're interested in learning more about this.

Take a moment to write a message to yourself about keeping on going, even when you're feeling ashamed, sad, unworthy, scared, and so on. I let myself feel my feelings, but don't let them decide what I actually do. I hope you can find some freedom too.

. . . .

. . . .

. . . .

. . . .

ACTIVITY: MAKE A MARK

Sometimes my mind is so full that it needs emptying. I do this by putting marks on paper, whether in words, drawings or a mix of both. This is about giving yourself permission to make any marks on paper, no matter what they look like. Having a non-judgemental moment that's between just you, the paper and the pen can be liberating.

Make any marks or draw whatever comes to your mind. Try not to judge yourself for whatever you draw or write – if you want to throw your paper away at the end, you're free to do that. Here are some prompts to help you get started, if you fancy:

☆ Draw lines that have the quality of your emotion. Are they rigid, wild, squiggly or feathery? Some of my angriest drawings are full of thick, sharp lines.

☆ Fill the paper with shapes or splodges of colour that you feel relate to your feelings. Some of my happiest pictures have a yellow, orange and pink glow.

☆ Draw an animal, creature, person or something from nature that resonates with your emotional situation. I mentioned my crow character earlier in this chapter.

☆ Write a word that comes to mind and illustrate it.

A common experience for people with a diagnosis of BPD is struggling to recall emotional states other than the emotional state you're currently experiencing: sometimes, it feels like the present emotion will never pass. If you're comfortable doing so, you could draw in a notebook (or stick your paper in), so that over time you build up a series of images. Looking back at them might remind you of your capacity to experience a variety of emotional states, even when the current one feels like it will go on for ever.

ACTIVITY: A BOX OF EMOTIONS

In 'Ocean', one of my poems about intense highs and lows, I wrote 'I am only this moment, / only this pain / I relive that timelapse shot of the anemone / over and over again.' This line captures how trapped I feel within an emotion, as if it were stuck on repeat and will never leave my mind or body. As we have already explored, emotions rise and fall like waves. However, at its peak it's easy to believe that this is the only way you have ever felt and will ever feel.

One thing that may help is to prepare a box of images, objects or words that depict a range of feelings and experiences you have had before – including light and joyful ones. Things you have enjoyed and moments when you felt connected to others and the world around you are useful. You could include photos of people or places, paper items like tickets or leaflets connected to places, pictures of favourite books or films, small objects or items from nature. When you're experiencing an emotional state that feels like it will never end, the items in your box can act as a reminder that you have felt differently before – and will feel differently in the future too. Take them out; look at them; hold them.

What could you put in your box?

. . . .

. . . .

. . . .

. . . .

. . . .

In the past, I looked at photographs and told myself a narrative of shame and disconnection; that the people in the photos hated me and would be happier without me. If you notice yourself in this situation, pause, try something different, and maybe return to it later.

☆ Changing intense emotions

Psychologist and founder of person-centred psychotherapy Carl R. Rogers wrote: '[T]he curious paradox is that when I accept myself just as I am, then I can change' (Rogers 1961, p.17). I have noticed in my life that accepting something is often the first step towards changing it. Similarly, I have noticed that acceptance-based approaches often create space for intense emotions to gently shift.

There are times, though, when change-based approaches are what's needed in the moment – and I want to share some of my favourites here. As I mentioned earlier, learning what approach to take in which situations takes time and practice. Different things will work for different people at different times so be gentle with yourself as much as you can. Keep an open mind and be creative as you explore what works for you in different contexts.

Worst-case scenario – and coping!

When I'm anxious, being told 'Everything will be fine', 'Don't panic' and 'Just forget about it' makes me feel more panicky. One of the reasons I love the 'Cope Ahead of Time with Difficult Situation Skills' as outlined in Dr Marsha M. Linehan's *DBT Skills Training Handouts and Worksheets* (2015) is that it fights fire with fire. The 'worst-case scenario – and coping' approach allows me to – temporarily – let my anxiety run wild. It also helps me feel more in control of situations that tend to make me feel out of control.

The 'worst-case scenario – and coping' approach is about vividly imagining being in your challenging situation with your fears taking place and then – here's the twist – what you will do to cope. For example, if you're really scared of going to the dentist, then it's about imagining being at the appointment and how it unfolds. It's about visualizing hearing the bad news you are fearing – and then rehearsing what you will do to cope effectively. For example, this could be taking some breaths, talking about your fears or asking for what you need. The process of imagining should last no longer than five minutes – you could use a timer on your phone.

The 'worst-case scenario – and coping' approach helps me for two reasons. First, when I enter situations that prompt strong emotions, I'm easily swept up by how I feel. I therefore tend to do things that help momentarily but make things more difficult in the long term. Second, there's no way I can 'just forget' my fears, so it's more effective for me to use my lively imagination to play out the scenario in my head and then how I would cope.

Here's space for you to work through a 'worst-case scenario – and coping'.

What is happening?

. . . .

. . . .

How are you feeling?

. . . .

. . . .

What are your fears?

. . . .

. . . .

How are you coping with these fears? What are you doing or saying?

. . . .

. . . .

How are you feeling as a result of coping with these fears?

. . . .

. . . .

Balance out emotions

In Chapter 1, we explored that emotions have functions, including communicating messages to ourselves (and others) and motivating us to act in certain ways. For example, feelings of disgust often compel us to move away from what disgusts us, and feelings of joy generally make us want to do more of what we are enjoying. I am not saying that we should not act on our emotions. Sometimes, it's absolutely the right thing to do. Emotions are there for a reason.

However, over the years, I've sometimes found it useful to balance out my emotions. For example, when I'm angry and frustrated I may want to shout, and this is generally not an effective (or fair!) way of communicating. I have learnt to act opposite to my anger by consciously making my voice softer and choosing my words more sensitively. When I'm feeling ashamed, I often want to apologize or cancel plans with people to avoid 'taking up' their time. Over the years, I've tried to act opposite to this shame by moving closer to the things or people I want to run from and speaking openly about my life.

Below is space for you to reflect on key emotions and how you could act opposite. Understandably, it can feel strange acting opposite to an emotion. After all, emotions exist to drive certain responses, such as running, hiding, seeking comfort or pushing back against injustice. With practice, I am confident that balancing emotions will feel easier for you.

Name of emotion: . . . .

What this emotion is urging me to do:

. . . .

. . . .

How can I balance out this emotion, if acting on it will not be helpful:

. . . .

. . . .

Name of emotion: . . . .

What this emotion is urging me to do:

. . . .

. . . .

How can I balance out this emotion, if acting on it will not be helpful:

. . . .

. . . .

Name of emotion: . . . .

What this emotion is urging me to do:

. . . .

. . . .

How can I balance out this emotion, if acting on it will not be helpful:

. . . .

. . . .

Name of emotion: . . . .

What this emotion is urging me to do:

. . . .

. . . .

How can I balance out this emotion, if acting on it will not be helpful:

. . . .

. . . .

A short distraction

Not too long ago, I was sobbing at full force – everything felt too much. My stress levels were through the roof, and I felt demands on me that I couldn't fulfil. I wanted to escape. My thoughts turned suicidal as they tend to do whenever I feel this level of overwhelm.

I knew I needed a break but felt I had no time or space to take the space I needed. I spoke with someone close to me, and they reminded me of the importance of taking time for myself away from my worries. I then felt able to take some time to do something relaxing and unrelated to my obligations or my goals. The short-term investment of time for myself prevented a very challenging panic attack and episode of anxiety-driven insomnia.

In DBT there is the idea of taking a 'mini holiday'. The idea is to take a timed break (depending on what you need and on your schedule) that won't impact your obligations or goals but will give a mental break from stresses and demands. As someone who is excitable but who can also become overwhelmed, I've found this concept really useful for helping me to prioritize rest. One of the ways I take a short break is to indulge my love of quizzes and crosswords. These divert my attention from my anxieties to something different, and I emerge feeling more able to cope. In fact, I strangely credit quizzes and crosswords, as well as some of my favourite video games, with getting me through some of the most anxious times of my life.

What could you do to give yourself a short break from any stresses, challenges or demands? For more information on this please see *DBT Skills Training Handouts and Worksheets* by Dr Marsha M. Linehan (2015).

ACTIVITY: ZOOMING OUT

When I was a child, I would lie down and 'zoom out', imagining soaring above my house, then my street, city, country, continent, earth until I was looking at the entire solar system and beyond. I felt giddy to think about how small I was in an unfathomably huge universe. I try to apply this idea of perspective when I'm having what my husband and I call 'a BPD moment'. For me, 'a BPD moment' is when I'm fixating on something, looking at it so closely that it feels enormous, when in reality it's one thing amidst a much wider context of events.

For example, a little while ago, I sent a message to a friend, and they didn't reply. This lack of reply started to feel enormous in my mind, obscuring all other thoughts. I kept checking my phone to see if they had replied to me and then checking their social media profile to see if they had blocked me (of course they hadn't, they had no reason to). I found it difficult to remember the hundreds of friendly interactions we've had over the time we've known each other. I found it hard to remember the many reasons why this friend may not have responded – being busy, being distracted, valuing space, not thinking I needed a reply, and so on.

Once I noticed how big this worry had become in my mind, I tried 'zooming out'. I acknowledged that I am one friend amongst many in their life; their phone is probably full of messages. They have many activities in their day, events in their week, thoughts, priorities in their life, and so on. Whilst it can be painful when responses aren't as quick as we would like (or what we want to hear), it's really important to keep perspective with relationships. That's not to say that a response is not important, but a reminder to contextualize what is happening.

In the circle below, draw or write a few words about your worry. Around this worry write or draw all the other things that are simultaneously taking place in your life. For example, my worry might be 'My friend is not replying to my message, maybe I overwhelmed them'. Around this worry, I could note down various other things that are happening in my life such as 'I'm learning how to cook better', 'I'm planning some day trips on my days off', 'My sister is coming to stay soon' or 'I've just begun a new project at work'. Perhaps writing or drawing all the other things you've got going on in your life might make your worry feel less all-consuming.

I hope this activity is helpful to you. If so, you may want to read about the concept of 'expanding awareness' in *DBT Skills Training Handouts and Worksheets* by Dr Marsha M. Linehan (2015).

One little thing

Sometimes, our schedules are challenging. Sometimes, life throws us curve balls, perhaps several at the same time. Maybe we feel unwell during an important week at work, or something breaks in our house when we need it most.

A helpful question I ask myself during times like these is: *What one little thing would make this easier?* Sometimes, the 'little thing' is an addition to your day. It could be as small as taking time to sit down and have a coffee with yourself before work, having a few quiet moments before a hectic day. Sometimes, the 'little thing' is something to take away from your day. I cook my simplest meals on my busiest days and keep my weekends empty on weeks I have to stay late at work. Whilst these things may be little, they can have a tangible impact on our ability to stay calm.

What little things could you add or remove from your day when life feels overwhelming? How could you create some mental space or reduce your expectations in order to feel less stressed?

. . . .

. . . .

. . . .

. . . .

. . . .

. . . .

. . . .

. . . .

. . . .

. . . .

. . . .

CHAPTER 4

Empowering Myself
(Even When I Feel Helpless)

When I was at university, I had moods that would skyrocket and then divebomb. The highs often related to what I was learning – I loved my degree studying literature from the Medieval period to the present day. I had teachers who inspired me, sharing their passion for the authors, poets and playwrights whose writing meant so much to me. I had also made friendships that felt so right it felt like alchemy. It was like the stars were aligning for me, everything I wanted was coming into sharp focus – then the desperate lows would glide in. I felt suicidal in these times, unable to manage the excruciating feelings I was having about myself, my life and how disconnected I felt from others.

Events that seemed small to others – someone not replying to a message or getting slightly harsh feedback in class – would break me. I could only sleep, hurt myself, cry or think about dying during these moments. And then something would happen – my phone would light up with a message, a friend would knock on my door to say hi or I would dig up some determination from within, swipe some lipstick and eyeliner on and cycle to the library – and I felt okay again. Life was this fragile and this frightening. I never knew when my next crisis would hit and whether I would even emerge with all life's pieces intact.

I was diagnosed with BPD during my final year of university. Depression and anxiety weren't cutting it for me as diagnoses anymore. I'd been seeing a particular therapist for about a year when she first suggested that the difficulties I was experiencing might be explained by something called borderline personality disorder, known as BPD for short. This was the first time I'd ever heard of it and hearing her say the words panicked me. What was this? Could this describe me? When I got back to my university halls, I googled it immediately.

The internet told me stories of people – almost exclusively women – who were chronically suicidal and always self-harming. These people were described as masterful manipulators, drama-queens addicted to attention; irresponsible individuals with no care for anyone else's feelings or any integrity in anything they did. I found countless articles with titles like 'How to spot borderlines', 'Five reasons why a borderline will ruin your life' and 'Why borderlines are the patients doctors love to hate'. I couldn't relate and – moreover – didn't want to relate. I didn't want to be associated with any of this. Yet when I read about the recommended therapies for BPD, they sounded ideal. Learn to regulate intense emotions. Tick. Live life without feeling suicidal and thinking about self-harm. Tick. Be able to withstand strong urges without acting impulsively? Tick. Feel less anxious and fearful in relationships? Tick. It all felt so relevant to me.

The first time a person hears about BPD is likely to be an important moment. How did you first hear about BPD? What were your initial impressions?

. . . .

. . . .

. . . .

. . . .

In my final year of university, my crises increased in frequency and severity. There were several times when mental health nurses from the Crisis Team and the Home Treatment Team visited me. I felt exposed and embarrassed, even though they weren't in uniform, but I wanted to take the opportunity to try to find out what was happening in my mind now I was in the mental health system. For a while I'd been wondering if I had bipolar disorder, but since my therapist had mentioned the words bor-derline personality disorder I was desperate to know more. All I needed now was a diagnostic assessment by a psychiatrist.

Navigating the system wasn't easy. I was removed from the waiting list for diagnosis without being told and sensed an unspoken reluctance from professionals to pursue a diagnosis at all.

When I finally managed to get an appointment for a full diagnostic assessment, the conversation itself was unremarkable, comprising the usual questions about my mood, thoughts and past experience. It was the end that jarred me. The mental health professional told me that I met the criteria for a BPD diagnosis, but didn't want to write this in my medical notes. The implication was that it was better if it was for my personal information only. Keeping it invisible will protect you, they seemed to suggest. The relief was immense as I stepped out of the consultation room – a name for what I was experiencing, an explanation of sorts. The possibility of finding a route through all this? But what did it mean that it was not going in my medical notes? And what was this unspecified danger that would happen if my diagnosis were to become visible?

☆ Difficulties following diagnosis
Misrepresentations

Having this new knowledge about myself but not knowing what to do with it scared me. I did what I did (and still do) best and took myself to the library. Libraries have always been comforting places for me. However, the books, articles and online videos I delved into told me everything I needed to know – about the stigma anyway. The imagery was shot through with violence and fragmentation: broken glass, shattered mir-rors, blood, fire, barbed wire and figures with two heads screaming. The pervasive colours were black and white, signifying extremity and inten-sity, alongside red to connote blood, anger, danger or sex. In the online articles and YouTube videos the 'crazy ex-girlfriend', 'bunny boiler', 'psy-cho-bitch' misogynistic tropes abounded. It seemed that every female celebrity who had died by suicide or had mental breakdowns in full glare of the paparazzi were casually labelled as 'borderline', as well as female on-screen villains and notorious criminals. This seemed to be all the more frequent if they were beautiful, and even more so if they were intelligent or talented.

I also saw that being a woman with BPD (or being 'borderline' as these women are often described) was to be stereotyped as hypersexual and cruel. The implication usually went like this: a 'borderline' will ensnare a romantic partner with the best (and the most) sex of their life, before wreaking havoc. The message was always the same: run a mile now – but you probably can't because you're caught under the spell. A 2010 article by Gina Piccalo entitled 'Borderline personality disorder and sex' captures some of these tropes. Piccolo writes that 'chaos can have a bewitching allure, particularly when it comes in the form of a whip-smart, dead-sexy woman with ferocious impulses, deep emotional scars and no real sense of self'. In this article, Piccolo names some of these 'dead-sexy women' as Marilyn Monroe ('a sex bomb who cloaked her own psychic wounds in breathy splendor'), Angelina Jolie's character in *Girl, Interrupted*, described as a 'terrifying mental patient' and Glenn Close's bunny-boiling character in *Fatal Attraction*. Perhaps the pinnacle of the misogyny I encountered was a YouTube video (which I believe has since been removed), depicting a 'borderline' as a zombie bride in the bath. The presenter of the video implied that the only way to remove a 'borderline girlfriend' from your life was to harm her with homemade weapons.

Have you encountered misrepresentations like these? How do they make you feel?

· ·

· ·

· ·

· ·

· ·

· ·

I could have avoided sharing such misrepresentations of BPD in an attempt to protect readers. I didn't, however, because I imagine you will already be familiar with them, and I wanted to call them out as dangerous – and inaccurate. Representations affect the way individuals construct images of themselves. When I was newly diagnosed, they skewed my image of myself at times and made me fear that I was truly a hideous monster, especially when I was feeling vulnerable or it was late at night and I felt alone. Frequently, though, I felt strong enough to think critically and acknowledge these misrepresentations as products of misogyny and prejudice. I felt anger that a group of people, often struggling deeply, were being portrayed in a false light and not being seen for who they truly are.

Scared to speak

Most of all, even when I didn't believe in their truthfulness, these representations made me frightened to be open about my diagnosis. I was terrified of being seen as dishonest, manipulative or dangerous. I was terrified I would be rejected by people I loved and have my dreams – like my desire to be a parent or my ambitions of working with children – snatched from me. I carried the diagnosis like it was a stain on my character that I had to hide. Concealing a key part of myself made me feel dishonest and like nobody fully knew me. As a result, all of my connections with people felt inauthentic. If a friend told me, or implied, they valued my friendship, it was marred with the thought *If only you knew, you wouldn't be saying that.* Even though I was loved, it never felt fully real.

Is this feeling of having to hide something you can relate to? How do you feel?

. . . .

. . . .

. . . .

. . . .

When the lack of authenticity reached peak discomfort and I decided to tell friends, I had to summon all courage. Even the name 'border-line personality disorder' elicited disgust: I had to do everything in my power not to vomit. The name felt too personal – like there was something defective about my personality – the core of my being, who I was as a person – even though I knew *personality* in psychiatry referred to patterns of relating to yourself, others and the world. Even the word *borderline* (referring to the group of patients that used to be described as being between psychotic and neurotic) had an uneasy air about it. It reminded me of things with an uncertain status and had disquieting connotations of being 'almost, but not fully something'.

When I finally managed to broach the truth with friends, the vulnerability of it all made me ache for days. Had I so-called overshared? Had I made them uncomfortable? Were they judging me for what I had said? Were they googling it and deciding they couldn't trust me? Would we ever be close again?

How do you feel about the name 'borderline personality disorder'? How do you feel about each of the three words? Does it help you to know that *personality* in psychiatry refers to patterns in relating to yourself, others and the world or does it just feel too personal, a word of too great an importance to attach to the word *disorder*?

. . . .

. . . .

. . . .

. . . .

. . . .

. . . .

BPD is referred to as 'emotionally unstable personality disorder' (EUPD) in the International Classification of Diseases. How do you feel about the name EUPD compared to BPD? Do you think re-naming it entirely would be helpful? If so, what would you suggest? Others have suggested 'emotional regulation disorder' or 'emotional intensity disorder'.

. . . .

. . . .

. . . .

. . . .

. . . .

. . . .

I didn't even tell medical professionals because I was scared how I would be treated. I didn't tell employers in case I was deemed incapable or untrustworthy when I knew the opposite was true. When I was in crisis, though, and found myself sobbing on the floors of A&E – hospital emergency departments – desperate for help, I would reluctantly tell the mental health professionals about my BPD diagnosis as a last-ditch attempt to get help. A few times, help came in the form of supportive conversations that helped me bear the agony until it passed. One mental health nurse spent a long time talking with me until I could start to relate to myself in that moment with slightly more compassion. She reminded me that I was worth more than the way I was feeling about myself and helped me decide to get through the night and the following day.

Sometimes, however, help didn't come when I asked for it, and I was met with coldness and even harshness. I saw how other patients were seen as the 'real patients', seen as worthy of kindness and support, whilst I was seen as a 'timewaster' – too 'self-aware' and even too 'highly educated' to be in need, or deserving, of help. When I was suicidal and very visibly, tangibly distressed, I was treated as disruptive and disgraceful. 'You're scaring the patients', I was told by mental health nurses in A&E. 'Leave now or we will call the police to remove you.' I don't think I've ever felt so worthless. At other times, rejections were almost laughable in their ignorance. One mental health nurse on a crisis line said to me: 'You have a family, a job, a degree, a boyfriend, you have everything. So why are you suicidal? Are you ugly?' One professional I saw in mental health services ended a consultation with 'Don't do anything silly' and then made a gesture to indicate self-harming. At this point, almost nothing shocked me.

I wanted to make space for you to write down your experiences. What sort of attitudes have you experienced from health professionals? How have these responses impacted how you felt or feel?

. . . .

. . . .

. . . .

. . . .

. . . .

. . . .

Have you been excluded from care or treated unfairly and judgementally in healthcare settings? Have you been able to access support and care when you needed it?

. . . .

. . . .

. . . .

. . . .

. . . .

. . . .

Stigma and discrimination

In his influential work *Stigma: Notes on the Management of Spoiled Identity* (1963) sociologist Erving Goffman defined stigma as an 'attribute that is deeply discrediting'. In other words, stigma is a facet of a person, something either visible or hidden, that can lead to a loss of respect or reputation when seen (if visible) or revealed (if hidden). The word *discrimination*, often used in similar contexts to the word *stigma*, generally refers to the unfair treatment of someone based on a characteristic, such as race, gender, sexuality or disability. If you are reading this, then the chances are that you, like me, have experienced stigma and discrimination in relation to your BPD. I wanted to give some time to reflect on this, because stigma has huge implications for how we feel about ourselves and our lives.

In 'Experiences of stigma and discrimination in borderline personality disorder', Stiles et al. (2023) identified five themes in the experiences of stigma and discrimination for people with BPD by analysing previous studies. The themes they identified were:

☆ 'Resistance from clinicians (withholding information)
☆ Othering
☆ Negative impact on self-image/esteem
☆ Hopelessness surrounding the perceived permanency of BPD
☆ Feeling like a burden.'

Even at first glance, these may feel familiar to you. I want to turn to these five themes below and use them to share some of my thoughts and experiences, before giving you space for your own reflections.

Before we do this, I want to acknowledge that there are people who undoubtedly experience more stigma and discrimination than others. As I noted in my first book, 'ethnic minority people, when compared to White British people, are more likely to report adverse, harsh or distressing mental health experiences and poorer outcomes when in contact with mental health services'. Stonewall's 'LGBT in Britain Health report' also highlights the inequalities that LGBTQ+ people face in health services, including mental health services. Participants in the report describe having been told by professionals that their sexuality or their gender expression are to blame for their mental health problems (Bachmann and Gooch 2018). According to research from the Scottish Transgender Alliance, 63 per cent of trans people had experienced a negative interaction, such as being belittled or ridiculed for being trans, within mental health services (McNeil et al. 2012).

At the back of this book there are resources which may be useful for individuals experiencing stigma and discrimination in relation to other aspects of identity in addition to their mental health difficulties. I also want to make it clear to anyone who invalidates the additional challenges that LGBTQ+ people (including trans people) and/or ethnic minority people with mental health difficulties face – I have no time for hate or judgement. Please educate yourself!

'RESISTANCE FROM CLINICIANS (WITHHOLDING INFORMATION)'

Many people diagnosed with BPD are not given enough information about their diagnosis. Furthermore, many are not informed about their diagnosis and find out incidentally, for example by overhearing professionals talking about them or incidentally seeing their medical records. This lack of transparency may seem shocking to people who haven't experienced this, but sadly it's not uncommon.

I feel strongly that individuals have a right to information about themselves and their health, and to know what clinicians are doing when interacting with them. Transparency and honesty should surely be at the heart of all branches of healthcare. The fact that a patient might (inconveniently) get upset or angry is not a valid reason for a clinician to hide a diagnosis. If a person is distressed and finding out about a diagnosis might distress them further, then a diagnosis should be shared at the earliest safe opportunity. I feel that people should be informed that a diagnosis is taking place and have the right to share their views and wishes on that. One of the pillars of medical ethics is consent and, as the UK's National Health Service website states, this means a patient must (where possible) give permission before they receive 'any type of medical treatment, test or examination' (NHS 2022). If this principle of giving permission is being respected, then nobody should be being diagnosed without being aware of this process.

I understand that occasionally there are exceptional circumstances, such as someone not having the mental capacity to understand this – and in these cases even more care and consideration for the individual's feelings should be taken. I wouldn't expect to be given a biopsy, X-ray, blood test or ultrasound, even if I was very unwell, without being told what was happening and agreeing to it, unless there was a very good reason I couldn't give consent and the test needed to go ahead immediately. So why are patients in mental health services being left in the dark about what is happening to them or what is being spoken and written about them? To me, it feels disrespectful and suggests a disregard for the power imbalance between professionals and their patients. It feels dehumanizing to be subject to something, especially without knowing, by someone who has power over you.

As I shared earlier in this chapter, I sensed a reluctance from professionals to diagnose me, perhaps because of the discrimination that can ensue or the difficulty accessing appropriate psychological therapies. I believe that the mental health professional who diagnosed me left this diagnosis out of my medical records because they wanted to protect me. What this did, however, was not protect me, but silence me and leave me with a suffocating shame. It's essential that clinicians work collaboratively with their patients in the spirit of openness – fully informing them of what is taking place in the room and facilitating a respectful dialogue that involves listening to concerns and exploring questions.

Have you experienced resistance from clinicians regarding diagnosis? Have you suffered a lack of information or a lack of openness and how did it affect you?

. . . .

. . . .

. . . .

. . . .

. . . .

. . . .

By contrast, have you experienced a willingness to listen and open communication from professionals about your care? What did this look like and how did it make you feel? If you haven't experienced this, what would this look and feel like for you?

. . . .

. . . .

. . . .

. . . .

. . . .

. . . .

. . . .

'OTHERING AND NEGATIVE IMPACT ON SELF-IMAGE/ESTEEM'

The term 'othering' describes the process by which individuals and groups are viewed, and treated, as different from and inferior to more dominant groups. Othering someone, or a group of people, involves alienating them from a larger group and signifying that they are unworthy of belonging and that others find it unpleasant to associate with them. Too often, people with BPD are othered in mental health services, health services in general, the workplace, within families and other aspects of society.

Within mental health settings, it's not an exaggeration to say that people with BPD are treated as the 'poor cousin'. Too often, mental health staff view people with this label as inferior to those with other, more compassionately viewed diagnoses. As I noted in my first book, a study on so-called 'difficult patients' in mental healthcare found that patients with a diagnosis of BPD were judged more negatively by staff than patients with other diagnoses, such as schizophrenia, even when their behaviour was the same (Koekkoek et al. 2006). The same study also states that when asked about the characteristics of 'difficult patients', psychiatrists mentioned BPD up to four times more often than any other diagnosis.

Similarly, in an evaluation of the 'effects of the label BPD on staff attitudes and perceptions', Markham found that mental health nurses 'expressed less social rejection towards patients with a diagnosis of schizophrenia and perceived them to be less dangerous than patients with a

BPD label' (Markham 2003). Interestingly, though, healthcare assistants did not show a difference of opinion on the same measures of 'dangerousness, social distance, optimism for change and ratings of personal experiences'. Markham also states that 'staff were least optimistic about patients with a BPD label and were more negative about their experience of working with this group'.

As McKenzie, Gregory and Hogg (2022) note in 'Mental health workers' attitudes towards individuals with a diagnosis of borderline personality disorder: A systematic literature review', 'the BPD label may elicit particularly negative attitudes because the term "personality disorder" can suggest that an individual is characteristically flawed'. They argue that the term does not provide information about a person's difficulties (e.g. problems regulating emotions or interpersonal struggles) or how these developed, and instead suggests the problem is located within their personality. If a mental health problem is conceptualized as something the person *is* (as BPD often is – 'they are a borderline') rather than something the person *has* (as PTSD tends to be – 'they have PTSD)', it is interesting to think about what impact that might have on how they are treated by others.

Does conceptualizing a problem as something a person *is* make it more likely for a professional to label distress as a character flaw *within* a patient ('They are just like that, ignore them!') and therefore see them as less worthy of care or even basic kindness? By contrast, does conceptualizing a problem as something happening *to* the patient make it more likely that a professional will act in a compassionate manner and to try to 'restore' them 'back' to health? There is so much to think about, with serious implications for how people are treated and their outcomes. I urge you to look into the research if you are curious.

I've already shared some of my more notable experiences of being treated as 'other', but some of these are harder to put my finger on. One of these, for example, is how mainstream mental health campaigns – think information posters on the walls in medical settings, charity campaigns, etc. – have never resonated with me. My difficulties don't fit with the more socially accepted, 'sanitized' versions of mental health difficulties that tend to be depicted or discussed. Let me ask you a question. How many TV documentaries have you seen about various mental health difficulties such as anxiety, depression, bipolar disorder? How many featured BPD? I imagine it will be no more than a couple and possibly zero.

Have you been or are you treated as 'other' and what was/is this like for you?

. . . .

. . . .

. . . .

. . . .

. . . .

. . . .

What would need to change for you to not feel 'other'? What would a sense of being included and belonging look like for you?

. . . .

. . . .

. . . .

. . . .

. . . .

. . . .

'HOPELESSNESS SURROUNDING THE PERCEIVED PERMANENCY OF BPD'

Lots of people with BPD feel there is no hope for them and believe that they will always struggle with an excruciating combination of intense emotions, immense anxiety in relationships, struggles with self-harm, suicide, and so on. This issue of hopelessness is complex. First of all, outdated beliefs about the permanence of these difficulties still pervade – perhaps linked to BPD being viewed by some (wrongly and dangerously) as an intrinsic character defect. Second, it's completely understandable to feel hopeless given the seriousness of these difficulties, especially in combination with struggles to access effective support and few stories of hope or positive representations of BPD in the media.

When I was younger, I was well acquainted with hopelessness. There were times when I felt nothing but a dark cave of despair inside myself, a black hole that I thought would suck me down until one day I could no longer fight its pull. It was not just hopelessness, but helplessness too. Seeing so many doctors and therapists, none of whom could fully help me or help me understand myself, made me feel broken. It was when I was finally offered DBT and met my life-changing DBT therapist, that hope came glimmering in. I realized I could learn how to regulate my emotions without hurting myself and manage my anxieties.

If you feel hopeless right now, there is no judgement from me, and I'm not forcing you to embrace hope. Hope cannot be forced anyway. However, my wish is that this book can bring some lightness to what can be a very heavy burden. With time, and with changes to your life and to how you relate to yourself and to others, I believe that your difficulties can lessen and life can start to feel easier. As I shared in my first book, there are a number of long-term studies that found most people with BPD 'improve with time' and that 'their prognosis is often better than expected' (Biskin 2015).

Take a moment to draw an arrow to show how you're feeling right now on the hopeless to hopeful continuum.

Hopeless	Neutral	Hopeful

Is your position on this continuum always the same or does it change depending on different factors such as time of day, who you are with and what you are doing? If your levels of hope change depending on different factors, is there anything you could do to have more of these and therefore bring more hope into your life?

. . . .

. . . .

. . . .

. . . .

. . . .

. . . .

'FEELING LIKE A BURDEN'

Feeling like a burden is a common experience for many people with a diagnosis of BPD. Feeling like an inconvenience to others and that anything you need – no matter how small – is too much is familiar to many. There was a time in my life when I would feel guilty for even walking over a pedestrian crossing because cars had to stop for me.

I felt like a burden for many reasons. First of all, I knew my difficulties were impacting on people who loved me. It was one thing for myself to feel pain, but to see my loved ones hurting in relation to my difficulties made me feel enormous guilt and shame. I felt hideous and berated myself for my difficulties creating pain for others. I would say things to myself like: 'How could you do this, Rosie? Look how you are making others feel? How could you be so awful?' Even though I never intended to upset people I loved, I punished myself for this nonetheless.

This feeling of being a burden was a key player in my suicidality – I constantly played with the idea that everyone would be happier without me. The thought went like this: *If everyone is unhappy with me, maybe they would be better off without me.* Then I would come to my senses and realize suicide would break people's hearts even more than they were already broken. This realization didn't make me happy, it made me feel so trapped I would cry for hours.

Even amongst some mental health professionals, who I thought were there to help, I felt like a burden. I described some of the difficult (and traumatic) events earlier in this chapter, but other experiences are harder for me to pinpoint why they made me so unsettled; experiences such as being labelled as 'complex', not fitting the referral criteria for certain services and being told I would have to pay a higher fee due to my diagnosis for private therapy.

The language used within mental health services plays an important role in how much of a burden an individual feels. Too often, people with BPD are incorrectly – and unfairly – described as 'difficult patients', being described as 'treatment resistant', 'refusing to engage' or 'rejecting help'. In 'Presenting complaint: use of language that disempowers patients', Cox and Fritz (2022) state that 'language is important' and that it affects relationships between professionals and their patients: 'In a medical context, language does more than transfer information between patients and healthcare providers – it has the potential to shape therapeutic relationships.' They go on to explain that 'specific word choices and phrases affect how patients view their health and illness, reflect healthcare workers' perceptions of their patients and influence medical care and treatments offered'.

Do you relate to feeling like a burden? Do you feel this across all areas of your life or certain areas only? Take a moment to reflect on your experiences.

. . . .

. . . .

. . . .

. . . .

. . . .

. . . .

The struggle to access support: Being 'at the margins'

I want to turn now to a key issue that is at the beating heart of what it means to be a person with this stigmatized diagnosis: the struggle to access the right support at the right time.

In 2003, the National Institute for Mental Health in England published guidance for the development of services for people with personality disorder. Its foreword states that the guidance 'brings this often neglected and isolated area of mental health into focus for the first time'. The guidance sets out some of the challenges faced by people with a diagnosis of personality disorder in accessing care and gives advice on the 'development of service models'.

The guidance, titled *Personality Disorder: No Longer a Diagnosis of Exclusion*, paints a bleak picture of unequal access to specialist services at the time of the document's publication. Responses to a 'questionnaire issued to all Trusts in England providing general adult mental health services in 2002', revealed that 17 per cent of them provided 'a dedicated personality disorder service', 40 per cent provided 'some level of service' '28 percent provided no identified service' and the remaining 15 per cent did not respond. The guidance described that 'many general mental health services struggle to provide an adequate service for people with personality disorder' and that people with these diagnoses are 'treated at the margins – through A&E, through inappropriate admissions to inpatient wards, on caseloads of community team staff who are likely to prioritise the needs of other clients and may lack the skills to work with them. It also states that 'many clinicians are reluctant to work with people with personality disorder because they believe that they have neither the skills, training, or resources to provide an adequate service'.

There has been much discussion online, in conferences and during training events about what has changed since the publication of *Personality Disorder: No Longer a Diagnosis of Exclusion*. I don't have access to data, but my sense is that there is still a very long way to go before there is equality between people with personality disorder diagnoses and those with other mental health diagnoses. 'At the margins' feels like an apt descriptor of where people with BPD often are. Overlooked. Sidelined. Shunned.

Have you struggled, or do you still struggle, to access support? Do you feel you are 'at the margins'? How does this make you feel? I hope reading this chapter helps you see this is not your fault, but part of a larger structural issue.

. . . .

. . . .

. . . .

. . . .

. . . .

. . . .

. . . .

. . . .

Personal views on a contentious diagnosis

Over the years, the debates surrounding BPD have made me feel like a key part of my identity has been a battleground. As I explored earlier in this book, it has felt, and still feels at times, complicated to occupy this space. I have friends who openly tell me they disagree with the diagnosis and feel it's harmful – I fully respect that and see the pain caused. Dr Jay Watts writes about why the BPD diagnosis 'remains among the most passionately disputed diagnoses in psychiatry' (Watts 2024). If you want to learn more about the harms caused, and perpetuated, by the diagnosis, I recommend exploring Dr Jay Watts's work.

Sometimes, I feel guilty and ashamed for embracing the BPD label as a name for my pain and an explanation for my suffering. Whilst I can certainly see the stigma, I can also see the flaws in the diagnostic concept itself – but I don't know if abolishing it is the answer. If the category of BPD disappeared, would the stigma be transferred elsewhere and continue to be applied to the individuals showing these same kinds of patterns of relating to themselves, others and the world? I also still feel the need for a word and descriptors to define my difficulties, and BPD reflects mine well. Whilst others do, I don't feel other diagnoses such as autism, ADHD or complex PTSD fit me. I don't have any concrete answers but am open to thinking about them as they matter. They matter deeply because there are people's lives at stake.

In 'Neuroqueer feminism: Turning with tenderness toward borderline personality disorder', Merri Lisa Johnson (2021) writes about BPD as 'a complex, historically misogynistic, yet still salient term for emotion dysregulation'. Johnson's 'analysis recasts personality disorders from the traditional medical classification as character defects to the less pejorative language of extreme or anomalous neurobiological states'. For Johnson the label still holds potential usefulness – in spite of all its flaws. I think this way of thinking about BPD is, for now at least, the one that sits most comfortably with me: I want the acknowledgment that comes from the label, but I don't want the label to call me 'damaged goods'.

In light of the various, often complicated and conflicting opinions about the BPD concept, how does this diagnosis sit with you? Overall, are you in favour of it or not? Perhaps you feel a mixture of ways about it. Do you want it abolished, re-imagined or something else? Perhaps you need time to think about it. Your opinions are allowed to shift; it's understandable that they may change over time.

☆ Facing the difficulties
The strengths of people with BPD

Acknowledging your strengths and the positive aspects of yourself is useful for everyone, but this becomes vitally – even urgently – important for people with a stigmatized diagnosis like BPD. It's clear to me people diagnosed with BPD have so many strengths and positives to share with others. In the last decade I've been privileged to get to know many people with a BPD diagnosis, some of whom became good friends. I've been lucky enough to experience first-hand their exceptional strengths and how much they bring to the world. Here are a few of the positives and strengths I have noticed that tend to be true of people with BPD.

Given the misrepresentation and negative attitudes that run rife across numerous contexts, the strengths of people with BPD can go unnoticed – except perhaps by those who know us most closely. I wanted to take a moment to share the strengths and positives I've noticed over the years as common characteristics amongst people with this diagnosis. Of course, everyone is different, but these are traits that seem to be often found in people with BPD.

REFLECTIVE AND THOUGHTFUL

People with BPD often seem to be reflective, thoughtful people who think deeply about themselves, others and the world. They may have insights into their emotions and those of others, perhaps as a result of their own process of trying to understand themselves. When their emotions are regulated, I believe people with this diagnosis may show a heightened awareness of difficulties that others may be going through as a result of learning about themselves.

NON-JUDGEMENTAL AND EMPATHETIC

It's my experience that people with BPD tend to be non-judgemental and empathetic towards others, especially people who are struggling or feeling 'at the margins'. I believe having experiences that are often misunderstood can make people with BPD less likely to form judgements about others before fully getting to know them.

I'm also often perceptive about others' emotions and thought processes, noticing their choice of words or even things they don't say. I place a high value on words and have always been drawn to reading and writing out of a need to understand myself and a curiosity about others' experiences.

People with this diagnosis may even appreciate the skill of being non-judgemental, empathetic and perceptive that it leads them to prioritize these in their life. I'm not aware of any research on this topic, but I believe that for these reasons people with this diagnosis are often found in caring and people-oriented professions like health, social care, teaching, psychology, and so on.

VALUING CONNECTIONS AND EMOTIONAL GENEROSITY

People with BPD are sensitive within relationships; but another way of looking at this is that people with this diagnosis tend to treasure their relationships. They tend to value their connections with people they love, placing a high value on friendship and family relationships. In my experience, people with BPD tend to be generous with their emotions, for example showing gratitude and affection freely, and often enjoy being there for people they love in any way they can. Whilst, at times, I've struggled with feeling embarrassed about these attributes in myself, I know that valuing relationships and being emotionally generous are beautiful qualities to bring to the world.

RESILIENT AND CREATIVE THINKERS

Having experienced life 'at the margins', people with BPD can become adept at making creative use of whatever they have at any given moment. I managed to teach myself some emotional regulation skills when I was on the waiting list for DBT as I was so desperate for anything to help. The level of resilience that people with BPD show to weather each emotional storm, sometimes day in day out, is astounding. I wish it didn't have to be so hard though. Getting praised by my therapist for doing DBT skills when I started DBT felt strange. I had been trying far harder to cope before I started this therapy, but the only difference was that I had far fewer successes to show for my efforts when I didn't know what I was doing.

COURAGEOUS

People with BPD display enormous amounts of courage – invisible courage – every day. Examples from my life are: being honest with a new professional (fear of judgement); disclosing BPD to a work colleague (fear of discrimination); discussing traumatic memories in therapy (fear of losing control of my emotions); making a new friend (fear of rejection); and publishing a book about BPD. Yet I have courage and do all of these things because it feels like the right thing for me. If you have BPD or experience stigma in any way, I bet you will know what I mean. So many writers and thinkers have put it more eloquently than me, but it takes courage to make yourself vulnerable.

Your strengths and positive attributes

Here's space for you to reflect on the wonderful things you bring to your relationships and to the world. I know it might feel uncomfortable, but I hope you will feel able to give it a try when the time is right. In the middle of the box draw a picture of yourself or stick a photo of yourself. Around your drawing or photo, note your strengths and positives using words or short phrases. Feel free to use the strengths and positives I shared above if they ring true for you, but also add your own if you want. There is only one rule with this: you're not allowed to write down negatives or anything that undermines the strengths and positives, for example, 'Other people say I'm empathetic, but maybe I'm not'.

Once you have completed this activity, why not draw it out in big on a piece of paper and stick it somewhere you can see it each day? The idea is to counteract the stereotypes and misrepresentations, giving way to a more accurate, affirming, empowering – and even celebratory – image of yourself! It has taken me many years to see myself in a positive light and now, most days, I can! I hope I can help you to feel the same over time.

CHAPTER 5

Connecting with
Others (and with Myself)

After sending my first book out into the world, and through writing this one, I realized that my experiences – described, imperfectly, as BPD – are relational at heart. My struggles are about how I relate to myself and about myself in relation to others. Accepting this has required courage. I feel vulnerable acknowledging that my emotions are contingent on the threads that connect me to others. I had to let go of the idea that it's random sparks misfiring in my brain that make me feel overwhelmed. I had to acknowledge that it's feelings of disconnection from people I care about that make me feel bleak.

But now I realize and accept that my struggles are relational in essence, I know why the moments that opened up the most space for me to become the person I am today were relational moments – moments of connection that I share with others. These moments are what make my life so fulfilling; stories swapped on an unrushed afternoon, laughter at the right time, the knowledge that someone else knows – as much as humanly possible – what it's like to feel this too. Perhaps this is why I built my career as a teacher, why I have such a strong bond with my daughter or why I treasure my friendships.

Do any of my experiences resonate with you? Can you think of any moments of connection that have meant, or mean, a lot to you? If not, what might having such moments in the future mean for you?

. . . .

. . . .

. . . .

. . . .

. . . .

. . . .

Embracing my contradictions

Moments of connection with others are precious in and of themselves. However, they act as a mirror, lighting up connections within myself too. For example, I used to think of myself as like two people in one body: one happy, one depressed; one in love with life, one suicidal; one with her head held high, one too ashamed to look others in the eye.

I no longer feel this way. The moments of connection I had with people who didn't turn away when I showed them the parts of myself that frightened me meant I could start to embrace my contradictions. The friends who were able to listen to stories from all corners of my life. My husband who didn't love me out of pity, but out of joy. My colleagues in education who knew about my diagnosis but never doubted my strengths. Let me share a few more examples with you with some questions to get you thinking.

The nurse who took time to understand

Several years ago, I was in A&E feeling suicidal and didn't know how to keep myself safe. Whilst waiting, I was nervous about how the staff would treat me given my previous experiences of being treated coldly – as if I weren't a 'real patient'. When the nurse arrived, she related to me with warmth and empathy. She spent a couple of hours talking with me about what had led me to feel this distressed and why it felt so difficult for me to go on living at that time. We had a conversation about who I was as a person, what was important to me, my hopes, how I wanted to feel and navigate the world. She understood how painful and overwhelming it was for me to feel everything with such intensity and how completely alone I felt with that.

By the time I had left the labyrinthine hospital corridors, she had opened up the thought in me that maybe I deserved to live. That maybe I *needed* to live – and that my difficulties could actually be my strengths. For the first time, I felt that it might be possible, very gently and very slowly, to find a way of being in the world that didn't hurt relentlessly.

Have you ever had someone listen to and see all parts of you, both struggles and strengths? What did it mean to you? If you haven't experienced this, what might it look like and how might it make you feel about yourself?

. . . .

. . . .

. . . .

. . . .

. . . .

. . . .

Taking the mic

I went to spoken-word nights regularly across London for a few years. On stage, I took the mic and shared my poems with a confidence that was new to me. I had conversations with strangers, some of whom became friends, about writing and what it meant to stand up and share it. During these nights, we used the stage to launch personal truths like little missiles: desperate to land on target. They usually did – these communities made it their mission to listen and be listened to, see and be seen. It felt like a sanctuary, an electrifying one, open to anyone who loved writing and who felt like the world judged them too much too fast.

At that time, I wrote ferociously as if I needed to do it to keep breathing. I'd spent years wanting to pull my tongue out of my mouth – 'You talk too much, think too much, love too much, are everything too much',

I told myself all the time. These communities accepted, and even celebrated, this in me. The moments of connections I enjoyed sparked the idea inside of me that maybe it was okay to be me, maybe it was even *good* to be me. It felt like coming up for air.

Do you have any places where you feel able to 'breathe' and be yourself – all of yourself? If not, are there any places that might offer this possibility that you could explore?

. . . .

. . . .

. . . .

. . . .

. . . .

. . . .

'You gave my child confidence'

I love my work as a teacher and the connections I've made with children and families have illuminated my life. When I was a trainee and a newly qualified teacher, I had some months that were exceptionally difficult. I spent many nights unable to sleep, crying for hours about how chaotic my emotions felt and panicking about how I would be able to teach the next morning. However, the children – how much I cared about them and how much they enjoyed my lessons – made it possible for me to get up each morning. I saw how much it meant to them to be taught by someone who cared and saw the best in them. At the end of the year, a parent approached me with tears in her eyes. She told me that I had given their child a gift: confidence. She didn't know how over the course of that year I had been struggling with my own feelings of worthlessness. She also didn't know how affirming it felt to know I had helped her child feel good in his own skin.

Around the same time, I had been volunteering on a listening line for children and young people who wanted a non-judgemental space to talk about their lives, anything from bullying, drugs and alcohol, exam stress, mental health, relationships, sexuality, and so on. The role felt strangely natural, and I was praised by the supervisors for how well I facilitated the conversations; after a while I was promoted to mentoring new volunteers. Outside of the shifts, I was struggling with my own desperate need to talk, write, do anything to make sense of myself. The irony was not – is still not – lost on me. I was giving others what I craved for myself.

Why am I sharing this? Too many people with stigmatized mental health diagnoses are throwing away their dreams of people-centred careers because they think they are too broken or too damaged. Yet, experiencing your own struggles doesn't mean you can't sit with someone through theirs. It doesn't mean you can't listen or think or relate. So long as I've had self-awareness and mindfulness that each person has a unique experience of the world, I've often been able to do these things fluently. In fact, getting to know other people's lives has been a privilege and has meant a great deal to me. Maybe one of the reasons for this is because I know much it has meant to me.

Can you relate to any of the above? Do you feel like you have skills in helping others, perhaps relating to your own experiences?

. . . .

. . . .

. . . .

. . . .

. . . .

. . . .

It's all the 'real me'

Today, I let my contradictions sit inside of me. I don't run from them anymore. Most of the time, but not always, I love them. I no longer try to work out which aspect is the 'real me' because they are all the 'real me'. This is me.

Do you feel contradictions within yourself that are difficult to reconcile with one another or hard to embrace? Write down the contradictions you feel, with the seemingly opposing ideas in different circles. In the overlapping part consider writing the word 'me', your name or perhaps drawing a picture of yourself if you would like to. You can be both aspects at once. Fragile and strong. Perfect and imperfect. Hurting and okay. Serious and funny. A talker and a listener. Caring for others and having others care for you. You don't have to be solely one or the other – I hope you find this concept as liberating as I do.

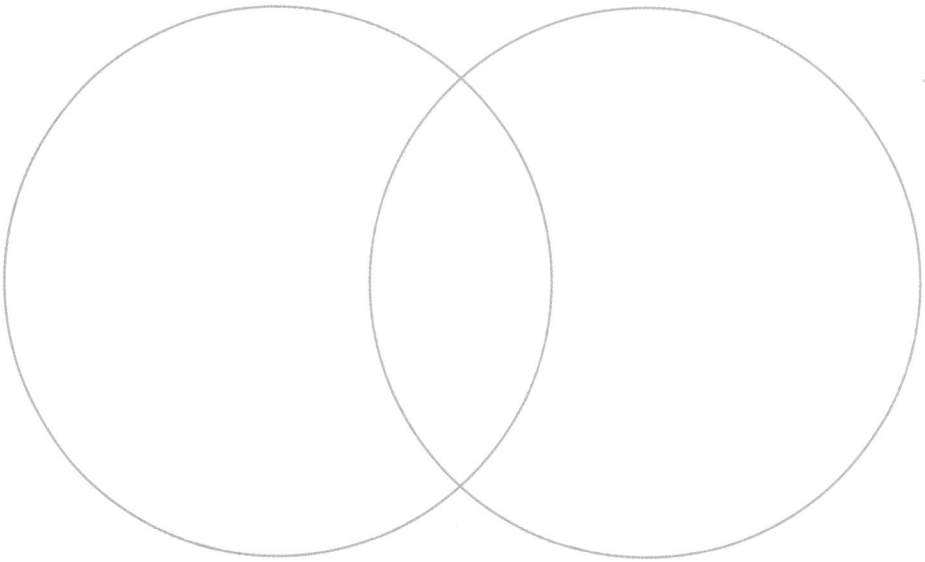

How do you feel about embracing your contradictions? Do you feel the same way as me – that all of these aspects might be the 'real' you?

. . . .

. . . .

. . . .

. . . .

. . . .

. . . .

☆ Feeling safe

In the last few years, I've had to think very carefully about who makes me feel safe. With whom am I safe to tell the truth about my life? Who won't judge me on a set of experiences before they get to know me? Who won't be scared or horrified by the facts of my life? It hurts to be a subject of embarrassment, disgust or fear simply for being who I am. If you're reading this book, I imagine you might relate.

Over the years, I've cultivated many relationships with people who make me feel safe – at home, in my friendships, at work, with professionals like psychiatrists and therapists and in other communities. These people don't respect me less for knowing who I am – they want to see the real me. Through conversations and self-reflection, I've figured out what makes me feel safe with someone:

- ☆ *Trust*: I need to trust that a person won't share what I tell them in confidence, unless there is a strong reason to tell someone else. I also need to know they won't use personal information to exert power over me or shame me. I don't want anything I shared to be used to embarrass me at a later date.

- ☆ *Complexity*: Since I was a child, it has been a complicated evolution to find the words that capture how I feel. The people I feel most comfortable talking about my life with are individuals who appreciate nuance and complexity. For example, people who appreciate that the words I'm choosing might mean something important to me and who understand that I might have multiple, possibly ambivalent, feelings about a single experience. I feel safest talking about my experiences with people who recognize that a conversation might be an exploration rather than the 'final word'. I also appreciate it when people are aware that not everything may have been said in the present conversation – and that there may be more layers to peel off at another time.

- ☆ *Open-mindedness*: I feel safest with people who are open to possibilities and recognize that everyone has their own perspective.

I don't feel comfortable with people who jump to conclusions or think they are the 'expert' on someone, especially if they haven't taken the time to listen and understand. I am most comfortable talking with people who embrace differences, rather than seeing them as something to fear.

☆ *Warmth and humour*: I find it easier to open up to people who are friendly and generous with their emotions. Also, just because I talk about aspects of my life that are painful doesn't mean I can't laugh about them too. Much of my relationship with my husband is built on humour. Laughing reduces my anxiety.

☆ *Relatability*: Many of my closest relationships are with people who have, for whatever reason, felt 'at the margins' but also remain aware that everyone's situation is unique. I tend to feel stronger connections more quickly with people who, like me, feel different in some way or who know what it feels like to be a subject of embarrassment, disgust or fear.

☆ *Honesty and openness*: In my closest relationships and friendships, I need to trust that the person will tell me if I've upset them. I tend to worry about whether I've overstepped boundaries or hurt someone, so being able to trust that they will tell me if something has upset them makes me feel safe. If there is a conflict, I value an open discussion rather than leaving it to fester in silence.

What makes you feel safe with someone? Make your own list and then reflect on which people in your life make you feel safe. If you don't have people in your life who make you feel safe, are there places you could explore to find these people?

. . . .

. . . .

. . . .

. . . .

. . . .

. . . .

☆ Celebrating myself?

Neurodiversity describes variation amongst people in how human brains take in, understand and respond to information. An individual described as neurodivergent has a larger difference in how their brain takes in, understands and responds to information. The neurodiversity paradigm is gaining momentum in many areas of society, transforming the way people think of themselves and others – and people are celebrating themselves and others for being neurodivergent more than ever before. It's had an influence on me since I published my first book.

I never dreamed I would be able to celebrate myself for what some people deemed feeling too much, crying too much, laughing too much, thinking too much, talking too much – being too much. I never dreamed I would be grateful for speaking about experiences some people told me to keep silent. I never dreamed I would appreciate aspects of my struggles as my strengths. I used to want to rip my tongue from my mouth and shrink my heart. Now, I want my words to take on their own lives without self-censorship, my heart to beat as loudly as it wants.

I don't always feel as confidently expansive as this though. Sometimes, I'm scared, and I have to reach inside myself – and towards others – to find the courage to open myself up over and over again. A constant unfolding. I ask myself questions, the same kinds of questions that I have asked you in this book. I open up space for myself to explore what I want and what I might need, from myself and from others.

When I was first diagnosed with BPD, I felt I couldn't ask for anything. I even felt that to exist in this world was to ask too much from it. I hope that through this book you can see that you are not too much and you're not asking too much – from yourself or from others. This book is words enclosed between two covers: close it up, put it on your shelf. But this book opens up too: its words – both mine and the words you have written

– contain possibilities, potential for expansiveness. So, whilst this book is still open, I want to ask one more question.

What would you ask from yourself and from others, if you knew you were deserving? After all you have been through – and all you still go through – you deserve nothing less than the utmost respect, support and understanding.

References

Agrawal, H.R., Gunderson. J., Holmes, B.M. and Lyons-Ruth, K. (2004) 'Attachment studies with borderline patients: A review' *Harvard Review of Psychiatry, 12*, 2, 94–104.

APA (American Psychiatric Association) (2022) *Diagnostic and Statistical Manual of Mental Disorders* (5th edn, Text Revision) (DSM-5-TR). Washington, DC: APA.

Babla, A. (2020) 'Putting the pieces together: Collage as a mode in the treatment of trauma.' https://collageresearchnetwork.wordpress.com/2020/05/29/putting-the-pieces-together-collage-as-a-mode-in-the-treatment-of-trauma

Bachmann, C. and Gooch, B. (2018) *LGBT in Britain – Health*. Stonewall. Available at: www.stonewall.org.uk/lgbt-britain-health

Bateman, A. and Fonagy, P. (2010) 'Mentalization based treatment for borderline personality disorder.' *World Psychiatry, 9*, 1, 11–15.

Biskin, R.S. (2015) 'The lifetime course of borderline personality disorder.' *Canadian Journal of Psychiatry, 60*, 7, 303–308.

Cavale, J., Chand Singh, D. and Hemchand, L. (2024) 'Male homosexuality and borderline personality disorder.' *Journal of Men's Health, 20*, 10, 32–51.

Cloud, J. (2009, 8 January) 'The mystery of borderline personality disorder.' *Time Magazine*. https://time.com/archive/6687374/the-mystery-of-borderline-personality-disorder

Cox, C. and Fritz, Z. (2022) 'Presenting complaint: Use of language that disempowers patients', *British Medical Journal, 377*, e066720

Dorfman, N. and Joel Reynolds, M. (2023) 'The new hysteria: Borderline personality disorder and epistemic injustice.' *International Journal of Feminist Approaches to Bioethics, 16*, 2, 162–181.

Dunlop, B.J. (2022) *The Queer Mental Health Workbook: A Creative Self-Help Guide Using CBT, CFT and DBT*. London: Jessica Kingsley Publishers.

Goffman, E. (1963) *Stigma Notes on the Management of Spoiled Identity*. Englewood Cliffs, NJ: Prentice-Hall.

Johnson, M. (2021) 'Neuroqueer feminism: Turning with tenderness toward borderline personality disorder'. *Signs: Journal of Women in Culture and Society, 46*, 3, 635–662.

Johnstone, L. and Boyle, M. (2018) *The Power Threat Meaning Framework*. Leicester: British Psychological Society.

Klein, P., Fairweather, A.K. and Lawn, S. (2022) 'Structural stigma and its impact on healthcare for borderline personality disorder: A scoping review.' *International Journal of Mental Health Systems, 16*, 1, 48.

Koekkoek, B., van Meijel, B. and Hutschemaekers, G. (2006) '"Difficult patients" in mental health care: A review.' *Psychiatric Services 57*, 6, 795–802.

Linehan, M.M. (1993) *Cognitive-Behavioral Treatment of Borderline Personality Disorder.* New York, NY: Guilford Press.

Linehan, M.M. (2015) *DBT Skills Training Handouts and Worksheets* (2nd edn). New York, NY: Guilford Press.

Markham, D. (2003) 'Attitudes towards patients with a diagnosis of "borderline personality disorder": Social rejection and dangerousness.' *Journal of Mental Health, 12*, 595–612.

McKenzie, K., Gregory, J. and Hogg, L. (2022) 'Mental health workers' attitudes towards individuals with a diagnosis of borderline personality disorder: A systematic literature review.' *Journal of Personality Disorders, 36*, 1, 70–98.

McNeil, J., Bailey, L., Ellis, S., Morton, J. and Regan, M. (2012) *Trans Mental Health Study 2012.* Edinburgh: Scottish Transgender Alliance. Available at: www.scottishtrans.org/wp-content/uploads/2013/03/trans_mh_study.pdf

Mulder, R. and Tyrer P. (2023) 'Borderline personality disorder: A spurious condition unsupported by science that should be abandoned.' *Journal of the Royal Society of Medicine, 116*, 4, 148–150.

National Institute for Mental Health in England (NHS) (2003) *Personality Disorder: No Longer a Diagnosis of Exclusion.*

NHS (2022) *Consent to treatment.* https://www.nhs.uk/tests-and-treatments/consent-to-treatment/

Piccalo, G. (2010) 'Borderline personality disorder and sex.' Daily Beast. www.thedailybeast.com/borderline-personality-disorder-and-sex

Piepmeier, A. (2009) *Girl Zines: Making Media, Doing Feminism.* New York, NY: NYU Press.

Porter, C., Palmier-Claus, J., Branitsky, A., Mansell, W., Warwick, H. and Varese, F. (2020) 'Childhood adversity and borderline personality disorder: A meta-analysis.' *Acta Psychiatrica Scandinavica, 141*, 1, 6–20.

Porter, H., Smith J. and Watts J. (2023) 'My personality is not disordered, and neither is my gender. Response to: Evaluation of personality disorders in patients with gender identity disorder (GID).' *Journal of Family Medicine and Primary Care, 12*, 6, 1245–1246.

Rodriguez-Seijas, C., Morgan, T.A. and Zimmerman, M. (2021) 'Is there a bias in the diagnosis of borderline personality disorder among lesbian, gay, and bisexual patients?' *Assessment, 28*, 3, 724–738.

Rogers, C.R. (1961) *On Becoming a Person: A Therapist's View of Psychotherapy.* Boston, MA: Houghton Mifflin.

Shaw, C. and Proctor, G. (2005) 'Women at the margins: A critique of the diagnosis of borderline personality disorder.' *Feminism & Psychology, 15*, 4, 483–490.

Stiles, C., Batchelor, R., Gumley, A. and Gajwani, R. (2023) 'Experiences of stigma and discrimination in borderline personality disorder: A systematic review and qualitative meta-synthesis.' *Journal of Personality Disorders, 37*, 2, 177–194.

Stonewall (2025) 'New survey findings reveal alarming scale of conversion practices in Great Britain.' www.stonewall.org.uk/news/new-research-reveals-alarming-scale-of-conversion-practices-in-great-britain

Sulzer, S.H. (2015) 'Does "difficult patient" status contribute to de facto demedicalization? The case of borderline personality disorder.' *Social Science & Medicine, 142*, 82–89.

Watts, J. (2016) 'Borderline personality disorder – a diagnosis of invalidation.' Huffington Post. www.huffingtonpost.co.uk/dr-jay-watts/borderline-personality-di_b_12167212.html

Watts, J. (2024) 'The epistemic injustice of borderline personality disorder.' *Lancet Psychiatry, 4*, 1, 23–24.

Support and Resources

Books

Aguirre, B. and Galen, G. (2013) *Mindfulness for Borderline Personality Disorder: Relieve Your Suffering Using the Core Skill of Dialectical Behavior Therapy*. Oakland, CA: New Harbinger.

Cappuccino, R. (2021) *Talking About BPD: A Stigma-Free Guide to Living a Calmer, Happier Life with Borderline Personality Disorder*. London: Jessica Kingsley Publishers.

Corso, D. (2017) *Stronger Than BPD: The Girl's Guide to Taking Control of Intense Emotions, Drama and Chaos Using DBT*. Oakland, CA: New Harbinger.

Corso, D. and Holt, K.C. (2018) *The Stronger Than BPD Journal: DBT Activities to Help You Manage Emotions, Heal from Borderline Personality Disorder, and Discover the Wise Woman Within*. Oakland, CA: New Harbinger.

Dunlop, B.J. (2022) *The Queer Mental Health Workbook: A Creative Self-Help Guide Using CBT, CFT and DBT*. London: Jessica Kingsley Publishers.

Linehan, M.M. (2015) *DBT Skills Training Handouts and Worksheets* (2nd edn). New York, NY: Guilford Press.

Blogs, vlogs and websites

Healing From BPD: www.youtube.com/user/HealingFromBPD

Talking About BPD (my website): www.talkingaboutbpd.co.uk

Support organizations and helplines
UK

Mind: www.mind.org.uk

Refuge: 0808 2000 247, www.nationaldahelpline.org.uk

Rethink Mental Illness: www.rethink.org

Samaritans: 116 123, www.samaritans.org

Shout: Text 85258, www.giveusashout.org

Switchboard: 0300 330 0630, https://switchboard.lgbt

USA and Canada

Crisis Services Canada: 1 833 456 4566

Crisis Text Line (USA and Canada): Text: 741741, www.crisistextline.org

National Domestic Violence Hotline (USA): 1 800 799 7233, www.ndvh.org

National Education Alliance for Borderline Personality Disorder (NEA-BPD) (USA): www.borderlinepersonalitydisorder.org

National Suicide Prevention Lifeline (USA): 1 800 273 8255, www.suicidepreventionlifeline.org

Sheltersafe.ca (Canada): www.sheltersafe.ca

Trans Lifeline (USA and Canada): 877 565 8860 (USA); 877 330 6366 (Canada), https://translifeline.org

Australia and New Zealand

Lifeline (Australia): 13 11 14, www.lifeline.org.au

Lifeline (New Zealand): 0800 543 354, www.lifeline.org.nz

OUTline (New Zealand): 0800 688 5463, https://outline.org.nz

QLife (Australia): 1800 184 527, https://qlife.org.au

1800 Respect (Australia): 1800 737 732, www.1800respect.org.au

☆ Finding a therapist
UK

British Association for Counselling and Psychotherapy (BACP) (UK): www.bacp.co.uk

The Black, African and Asian Therapy Network (BAATN) (UK): www.baatn.org.uk

Pink Therapy (UK): www.pinktherapy.com

UK Council for Psychotherapy (UKCP) (UK): www.psychotherapy.org.uk

USA and Canada

Canadian Mental Health Association (CMHA) (Canada): https://cmha.ca/find-your-cmha

Mental Health America (MHA) Affiliate Resource Centre (USA): https://mhanational.org/arc

Australia and New Zealand

Australia Counselling (Australia): www.australiacounselling.com.au/find-a-therapist

Healthline (New Zealand): 0800 611 116

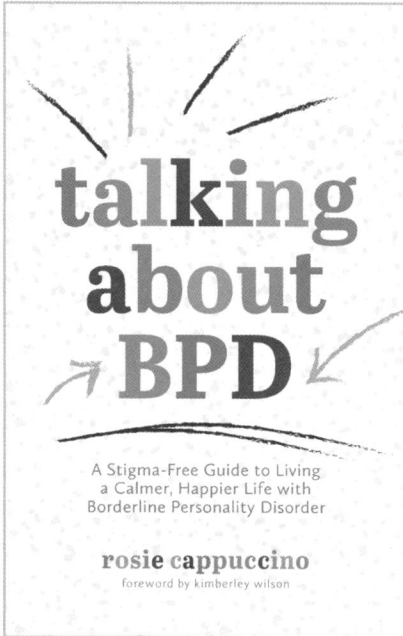

Talking About BPD

A Stigma-Free Guide to Living a Calmer, Happier Life with Borderline Personality Disorder
Rosie Cappuccino
Foreword by Kimberley Wilson
ISBN 978 1 78775 825 4
eISBN 978 1 78775 826 1

A self-help guide to life with Borderline Personality Disorder from award-winning blogger Rosie Cappuccino. Over 6,000 copies sold!

'I am Rosie. I have BPD. I am not an attention-seeker, manipulative, dangerous, hopeless, unlovable, "broken", "difficult to reach" or "unwilling to engage". I am caring, creative, courageous, determined, full of life and love.'

Talking About BPD is a positive, stigma-free guide to life with borderline personality disorder (BPD) from award-winning blogger Rosie Cappuccino.

Addressing what BPD is, the journey to diagnosis and available treatments, Rosie offers advice on life with BPD and shares practical tips and DBT-based techniques for coping day to day. Topics such as how to talk about BPD to those around you, managing relationships and self-harm are also explored. Throughout, Rosie shares her own experiences and works to dispel stigma and challenge the stereotypes often associated with the disorder.

This much-needed, hopeful guide will offer support, understanding, validation and empowerment for all living with BPD, as well as those who support them.

RAISING READERS
Books Build Bright Futures

Dear Reader,

We'd love your attention for one more page to tell you about the crisis in children's reading, and what we can all do.

Studies have shown that reading for fun is the **single biggest predictor of a child's future life chances** – more than family circumstance, parents' educational background or income. It improves academic results, mental health, wealth, communication skills, ambition and happiness.[1]

The number of children reading for fun is in rapid decline. Young people have a lot of competition for their time. In 2024, 1 in 10 children and young people in the UK aged 5 to 18 did not own a single book at home.[2]

Hachette works extensively with schools, libraries and literacy charities, but here are some ways we can all raise more readers:

- Reading to children for just 10 minutes a day makes a difference
- Don't give up if children aren't regular readers – there will be books for them!
- Visit bookshops and libraries to get recommendations
- Encourage them to listen to audiobooks
- Support school libraries
- Give books as gifts

There's a lot more information about how to encourage children to read on our website: **www.RaisingReaders.co.uk**

Thank you for reading.

hachette
UK

---

1   OECD, '21st-Century Readers: Developing Literacy Skills in a Digital World', 2021, https://www.oecd.org/en/publications/21st-century-readers_a83d84cb-en.html

2   National Literacy Trust, 'Book Ownership in 2024', November 2024, https://literacytrust.org.uk/research-services/research-reports/book-ownership-in-2024